Taj Mahal p71
Buza I / II pp60/61
The walls pp 34-37
Stradun - main street at night pp 58/59

Korcula - p 125
Lopud?
Luza Square p54
    music/ singing/ dancing.

Time Out

SHORTLIST

Dubrovnik

WHAT'S NEW | WHAT'S ON | WHAT'S BEST

www.timeout.com/dubrovnik

D0180567

Time Out
Croatia

Contents

Published by Time Out Guides Ltd
Universal House
251 Tottenham Court Road
London W1T 7AB
Tel: + 44 (0)20 7813 3000
Fax: + 44 (0)20 7813 6001
Email: guides@timeout.com
www.timeout.com

Managing Director Peter Fiennes
Editorial Director Ruth Jarvis
Deputy Series Editor Dominic Earle
Business Manager Gareth Garner
Guides Co-ordinator Holly Pick
Accountant Kemi Olufuwa

Time Out Guides is a wholly owned subsidiary of Time Out Group Ltd.

© Time Out Group Ltd
Chairman Tony Elliott
Financial Director Richard Waterlow
Time Out Magazine Ltd MD David Pepper
Group General Manager/Director Nichola Coulthard
Managing Director, Time Out International Cathy Runciman
Time Out Communications Ltd MD David Pepper
Production Director Mark Lamond
Group Marketing Director John Luck
Group Art Director John Oakey
Group IT Director Simon Chappell

Time Out and the Time Out logo are trademarks of Time Out Group Ltd.

This edition first published in Great Britain in 2007 by Ebury Publishing
A Random House Group Company
Company information can be found on www.randomhouse.co.uk
10 9 8 7 6 5 4 3 2 1

For details of distribution in the Americas, see www.timeout.com

ISBN 13: 978184670 0408
ISBN 10: 1-84670-040-X

A CIP catalogue record for this book is available from the British Library

Printed and bound by Firmengruppe APPL, aprinta druck, Wemding, Germany

The Random House Group Limited makes every effort to ensure that the papers used in
our books are made from trees that have been legally sourced from well-managed and
credibly certified forests. Our paper procurement policy can be found on
www.randomhouse.co.uk

Dubrovnik Shortlist

The **Time Out Dubrovnik Shortlist** is one of a new series of guides that draws on Time Out's background as a magazine publisher to keep you current with what's going on in town. As well as the key sights and the best of Dubrovnik's eating, drinking and leisure options, the guide picks out the most exciting venues to have arrived, and gives a calendar of annual events. It also includes features on new trends and openings, compiled by locally based editors and writers. Whether you're visiting for the first time, or you're a regular, you'll find the *Time Out Dubrovnik Shortlist* contains all you need to know, in a portable and easy-to-use format.

The guide divides Dubrovnik into five areas, each of which contains listings for Sights & Museums, Eating & Drinking, Shopping, Nightlife and Arts & Leisure, with maps pinpointing all their locations. At the front of the book are chapters rounding up these scenes city-wide, and giving a shortlist of our overall picks in a variety of categories. We include itineraries for days out, plus essentials such as transport information and hotels.

Our listings use phone numbers as dialled within Croatia. In Dubrovnik, drop the 020 code. From abroad, dial your access code, then 385 for Croatia, then the number given, dropping the initial '0'. Some listed numbers (usually 098 or 091) are mobiles, indicated as such. From a UK mobile, call 00 385, then the rest of the number, minus the initial '0'. Mobile calls can be expensive.

We have given hotel listings in price categories, using one to four euro signs (€-€€€€), representing budget, moderate, expensive and luxury. Major credit cards are accepted unless otherwise stated. All of our listings are double-checked, but places can close or change their hours or prices, so it's a good idea to call a venue before visiting. While every effort has been made to ensure accuracy, the publishers cannot accept responsibility for any errors that this guide may contain.

Venues are marked on the maps using symbols numbered according to their order within the chapter and colour-coded according to the type of establishment they represent:

- ❶ Sights & Museums
- ❶ Eating & Drinking
- ❶ Shopping
- ❶ Nightlife
- ❶ Arts & Leisure

SHORTLIST
Online

The *Time Out Dubrovnik Shortlist* is as up to date as it is possible for a printed guidebook to be. And to keep it completely current, it has a regularly updated online companion, at **www.timeout. com/dubrovnik**. Here you'll find news of the latest openings and exhibitions, as well as picks from visitors and residents – ideal for planning a trip. Time Out is the city specialist, so you'll also find travel information for more than 100 cities worldwide on our site, at www.timeout.com/travel.

Time Out Dubrovnik Shortlist

EDITORIAL
Editor Peterjon Cresswell
Copy Editor Charlotte Thomas
Researcher Vesna Marić
Proofreaders Deborah Nash, Cathy Limb

STUDIO
Art Director Scott Moore
Art Editor Pinelope Kourmouzoglou
Senior Designer Josephine Spencer
Graphic Designer Henry Elphick
Junior Graphic Designer Kei Ishimaru
Digital Imaging Simon Foster
Ad Make-up Jenni Prichard
Picture Editor Jael Marschner
Deputy Picture Editor Tracey Kerrigan
Picture Researcher Helen McFarland

ADVERTISING
Sales Director/Sponsorship Mark Phillips
International Sales Manager Fred Durman
International Sales Consultant
  Ross Canadé
Advertising Sales Time Out Croatia:
  David Plant, Vanda Vučičević, Maja
  Bosnić, Dino Zulumović, Darko Perojević
Advertising Assistant Kate Staddon

MARKETING
Marketing Manager Yvonne Poon
**Sales & Marketing Director, North
America** Lisa Levinson
Marketing Designer Anthony Huggins

PRODUCTION
Production Manager Brendan McKeown
Production Co-ordinator Caroline Bradford

CONTRIBUTORS
This guide was researched and written by Peterjon Cresswell, David Plant, Goran
Vuković, Danilo Mitrović, Jane Cody, Gorana Jerković, Darko Perojević and Mirza Redzić.

PHOTOGRAPHY
All photography by Rajko Radovanović, except: pages 2 (top left), 3 (top left), 30, 122,
127 Rafael Estefania; p3 (top right) Hotel Bellevue; p3 (bottom right) Valamar Club Hotel;
p104 Jure-Zlatko Vujević/Bav-Adria Yachting; p124 www.adriatica.net.

The following images were provided by the featured establishments/artists: pages 66,
75, 98, 112, 133, 138, 148.

Cover photograph: Dubrovnik Old Town, Credit: Danny Lehman/Corbis.

MAPS
John Scott, JS Graphics (john@jsgraphics.co.uk).

Thanks to Marc and family, Goran V, Darko P, Vesna M, Andro Vidak, Toni Lučić
(Libertas), Nikolina Vicelić (ALH), Irina Ban and Dubravko (Visit Dubrovnik).

Special thanks to Time Out Croatia. Directors David Plant and Vanda Vučičević.

About Time Out

Founded in 1968, Time Out has expanded from humble London beginnings into the
leading resource for those wanting to know what's happening in the world's greatest
cities. As well as our influential what's-on weeklies in London, New York and Chicago,
we publish more than a dozen other listings magazines in cities as varied as Beijing and
Mumbai. The magazines established Time Out's trademark style: sharp writing, informed
reviewing and bang up-to-date inside knowledge of every scene.

Time Out made the natural leap into travel guides in the 1980s with the City Guide
series, which now extends to over 50 destinations around the world. Written and
researched by expert local writers and generously illustrated with original photography,
the full-size guides cover a larger area than our Shortlist guides and include many more
venue reviews, along with additional background features and a full set of maps.

Throughout this rapid growth, the company has remained proudly independent, still
owned by Tony Elliott nearly four decades after he started Time Out London as a single
fold-out sheet of A5 paper. This independence extends to the editorial content of all our
publications, this Shortlist included. No establishment has been featured because it has
advertised, and no payment has influenced any of our reviews. And, for our critics,
there's definitely no such thing as a free lunch: all restaurants and bars are visited and
reviewed anonymously, and Time Out always picks up the bill.
For more about the company, see www.timeout.com.

Don't Miss

Rector's Palace p57

Sights & Museums

A living museum piece in itself, Dubrovnik has plenty of mixed historic attractions but no absolute must-see building. What people come for is what is all around them, the **Old Town**, a UNESCO World Heritage site of its own, and the **City Walls** that surround it.

To get the best view of either, take a walking tour of the City Walls (pp34-37 **Itineraries**). There are three access points, the main one by the **Pile Gate**.

Everything in and around the Old Town is walkable. Few sights are more than ten minutes away from each other. The only trek is to scale **Mount Srdj**, a feat whose reward is the fabulous view rather than the ruins of Napoleon's fort and the cable-car station here.

The Old Town

Down below, the most notable buildings are grouped around the main square, **Luža**. The **Rector's Palace** and **Sponza Palace** are both attractive, with a number of historic artefacts, but none of them breathtaking. The two most prominent churches here, the **Cathedral** and **St Blaise**, both suffered significant damage in the earthquake of 1667 and the resultant reconstructions are somewhat bland. Luža contains a **clock tower** and **Orlando's Column**, both photogenic – but these somewhat light sightseeing duties lend themselves to lazy late mornings which might be more enjoyably spent at one of the many terrace cafés by the square.

Likewise, the adjoining main street of **Stradun** contains only shops and cafés, with Dubrovnik's mixed bag of museums and galleries mostly tucked away down its sidestreets. It is bookended by the Pile Gate, before which stands **Onofrio's Fountain**, and the religious sights of the **Franciscan Monastery** and **Museum**, and **St Claire's Convent**, facing each other. The former is extremely popular, mainly because of its unexpected, tranquil courtyard, and working **pharmacy**.

Dotted around the Old Town are an eclectic selection of sights, easily enough to fill any rainy afternoon. Don't miss **War Photo Limited**, a gallery showing scenes of recent global conflicts captured by some of the world's most acclaimed photojournalists. For fine-art photography, there's the recently opened **Carmel Photo Gallery**.

Within easy reach of each other, you can visit a working **mosque**, **synagogue**, **Orthodox Church** (as well as its modest, **Icon Museum**) and a dozen **Catholic churches**. Of the museums, the two most fun are the **Rupe Ethnographic Museum** – also offering a fabulous view of the Old Town – and the **House of Marin Držić**, an unintentionally kitsch look at the life and work of Dubrovnik's most renowned playwright from the golden age.

The two sights housed in **St John's Fortress**, at the **old harbour** end of the Old Town, are little to write home about, but add a pleasant interlude to a wander around the bobbing boats: the **Maritime Museum** and a somewhat dilapidated **Aquarium**.

Around Ploče

As you climb up from the old harbour towards the **Ploče Gate**, there are a handful of artistic

DON'T MISS

attractions in the **Dominican Monastery**. The key artist to look out for here is **Vlaho Bukovac**, the main Croatian figure from the late 19th century. Trained in Paris in the 1880s, Cavtat-born Bukovac also has many landscapes and portraits in the **Dulčić, Masle, Pulitika Gallery** by the Rector's Palace and, most significantly, in the unfortunately often overlooked **Museum of Modern Art** the other side of the Ploče Gate, past the public beach. It's really worth visiting this former Banac Mansion if you can. For one, it's an easy, pleasant walk from the Ploče Gate – you could even combine it with a couple of hours' sunbathing – and secondly, it offers the best of 20th-century Croatian art, in the quite wonderful surroundings of this converted house.

A further incentive comes in the form of **Lazareti**, just next to the Museum of Modern Art. A former quarantine barracks, it provides the atmospheric setting for a gallery workshop, DJ club, live-music venue and crafts centre.

Around Pile

The crumbling villas, neglected cemeteries and balustraded views of the sea crashing against the rocks below will form the bulk of your impressions of any steep wander around Pile and adjoining neighbourhoods of Boninovo and Kono. A couple of little known gems are definitely worth a detour.

Our Lady of Danče, also known as the Church of St Mary, contains a 1517 triptych, the last work by the most renowned painter of the Dubrovnik School, Nikola Božidarević. The church forms part of a nunnery – nuns still ring the bell to greet passing ships. A contemplative hour's wander to the church could easily include a visit to the wild, rocky beach below.

The better known beach here is **Šulići**, accessed via the photogenic street of **Od Tabakarije**.

Nearby **Gradac Park** offers a rare patch of greenery, laid out with Habsburg refinement. It's pretty rundown these days, but a decent spot to relax for half-an-hour.

High above looms Mount Srdj. Bitterly fought over by Napoleon's troops and Montenegrins in the early 1800s, and Serbs and Croats in the early 1990s, it was once the station for a scenic cable-car ride over Dubrovnik. You can still scale it today, provided you're fit enough for a two-hour climb starting at the Pile Gate. Be sure to take plenty of water if you're attempting this in the height of summer.

Orthodox Church p55

Sponza Palace p58

Gundulićeva poljana market

Eating & Drinking

Despite the fact that the lion's share of its economy is based on tourism, Dubrovnik's dining scene can be rather disappointing. The local perception of tourism is stuck in a 1970s' time warp. There is little variation in cuisine, and repeat custom is rare.

This is not to say you are always bound to get a bad meal in Dubrovnik. The town has a handful of very good restaurants. The trouble is that these select few tend to charge Paris prices for what is simply above-average cuisine in, admittedly, stellar surroundings.

The problem is not a lack of ingredients. Go to the local markets at **Gundulićeva poljana** or, better still, **Gruž**, and you'll find fresh greens, tomatoes, olives, peppers and cheeses, all grown or produced naturally and locally. A daily fish market is just around the corner. What you find on the average dining table at home can sometimes surpass what you might be served at one of the many average restaurants. A local has time to root out the best products; the average restaurateur is limited by sky-high rents and thin profit margins, shortage of storage space and lack of delivery access. Not all the fish you will be served will be fresh. Salads in many venues are lacklustre. The best oil is not always the one to be used.

Staffing is another problem. With so many venues competing for trade in one tiny space, diligent, loyal staff can be hard to come by.

The visitor can easily get the feeling that everyone in the restaurant trade has a few short weeks to make their money for the year – and make it they will.

Nowhere are these negative impressions more prevalent than in the Old Town – fortunately also the location for the few mould-breaking eateries to have opened recently.

The Old Town

Before the arrival of a handful of notable venues in the last four years, dining in the historic centre was typified by **Prijeko**. Here, down a long street parallel to Stradun, tourist-trap restaurants display unappealing photographs of the dishes they serve – and little tact. Barkers work the street corners of Stradun, trying to entice tourists up. For a town of Dubrovnik's stature, it's quite frankly an embarrassment.

Still, right here on Prijeko, the newly opened **Wanda** is setting standards. This well-staffed, buzzy venue offers simple, flavourful Mediterranean cuisine. Around the corner, the **Dubrovački kantun** makes the best use of greens from Konavle and locally grown herbs. In 2006, **Sapur** was easily the best table in town, its menu delving into historic regional dishes, until a management dispute saw it close that winter. The fact that it could have become so popular, with not even a sign on its door, speaks volumes. In all three cases, repeat business, word of mouth and personal recommendations saw tables occupied all summer.

Stiff, traditional establishments, such as **Proto**, still do a good trade. You'll pay a fortune and the formal surroundings may not engender a relaxing evening, but standards are high. This is why there are queues around the old harbour every day in summer

SHORTLIST

Best new spots
- Blidinje (p111)
- Spice Lounge (p117)
- Vapor (p118)
- Wanda (p72)

Best for breakfast
- Dubrava (p63)
- Festival Café (p64)
- fresh* (p64)

Best terraces
- Atlas Club Nautika (p95)
- Buža I (p60)
- Buža II (p61)
- La Caravelle (p84)
- Defne (p63)
- Kavana Dubravka (p96)
- Levanat (p114)
- Lokanda Peskarija (p67)
- Orhan (p96)
- Orsan Yacht Club (p117)
- Poklisar (p68)
- Taverna Arsenal (p71)
- Victoria Restaurant (p88)

Best for vegetarians
- Arka (p60)
- Dubrovački kantun (p63)
- Defne (p63)
- Taj Mahal (p71)
- Vapor (p118)

Best cocktails
- La Bohème (p95)
- East-West (p87)
- Hemingway Bar (p64)
- Spice Lounge (p117)
- Sunset Lounge (p118)

Classic Dubrovnik
- Festival Café (p64)
- Kavana Dubravka (p96)
- Proto (p69)
- Tovjerna Sesame (p97)
- Troubadour (p71)

Best local bars
- Libertina (p67)
- Ludwig (p67)
- Mališ (p102)
- Roxy (p117)

outside the **Lokanda Peskarija**, where diners pay 100kn-150kn a head for good, local cuisine served by a friendly staff in an informal, picturesque setting. No hard sell, no flimflam, no add-ons.

Around Dubrovnik

Most of the top tables outside the Old Town are at high-end hotels. Kitchens such as **Vapor** at the Hotel Bellevue, **Porat** at the Hilton and the **Taverna Rustica** at the Hotel Excelsior produce equally high-class, often fusion Med dishes to an international standard – at international prices. Exceptions are clustered around Pile – **Orhan** offers a fabulous setting, **Tovjerna Sesame** local ambience. The **Atlas Club Nautika** is, without question, excellent but under the same umbrella as Proto. Formal dining, fancy prices. Mention must also be made of the **Levanat**, the best option in Lapad for location and local cuisine, and the recently opened and promising **Blidinje**.

Outside Dubrovnik

Much fuss is made of **Konavle**. The garden of the Dubrovnik region, it's a folklorish area of fertile land at Croatia's far south, squeezed between the sea and the Bosnian and Montenegrin borders. Tour parties and locals beat a path to the door of its traditional, rustic restaurants for gastronomic delights prepared *ispod peke*; braised 'under a bell' with hot coals. The process takes a couple of hours so you should order when you phone ahead to book a table. Veal is a speciality but lamb and octopus are also popular.

Konavle's classic venue is the Konavoski dvori near the village of Gruda but you'll get an equally enjoyable experience, and better value for money, at the **Konoba Konavoski komin**, near Cavtat.

Menus & prices

Menus are are often very similar in many places. All (certainly in the Old Town) will have English translations, and begin by listing ubiquitous starters of Dalmatian ham or sheep's cheese, or fish or beef soups. There will then be a list of *gotova jela*, prepared dishes, typically risottos (black with squid ink is standard), standard pasta and so on. *Jela po narudžbi* or *specijaliteti* are house specialities. This will usually involve some kind of sauce; the tomato-based *buzara* is the most common in Dalmatia.

Grilled dishes (*na žaru* or *sa roštilja*) include meat (often lamb), fish (ask what's fresh that day – dentex, *zubatac*, can be excellent) and seafood. Squid, *lignje*, is on almost every menu. Beware that scampi, *škampi*, are served in their shells and not neatly manufactured in breadcrumbs. Shellfish from nearby Ston, particularly oysters, *kamenice*, can be excellent. Seafood may be garnished with *blitva*, a local kale, and potatoes. Salads include one made with *hobotnica*, octopus. The better kitchens will make use of rocket, *rokula*, grown here almost all year round. The classic Dalmatian dessert is *rožata*, a kind of crème caramel.

All staff will speak at least reasonable restaurant English.

In the Old Town, you'll be lucky to pay less than 200kn per head, excluding drinks, although travellers on a budget can usually order a simple prepared dish and glass of house wine for 75kn. By the bottle, it is usually sold at under 100kn; you will be paying twice or three times that for a good label. Away from the Old Town, prices drop considerably and many places offer locals a *marenda*, a cheap daily two- or three-course meal. These can be as little as 35kn.

Tipping is the usual ten per cent you add to the bill – or round off to a convenient figure. Many places impose a nominal cover charge. Places on Prijeko, and other tourist traps, try and make money on extras – you'll be charged for the bread and pâté that come before your starter arrives, for example.

Wine & drinks

The best regional wines come from Pelješac, in particular the ruby red **Dingač** from the southern slopes of this peninsula a short drive north of Dubrovnik. **Postup** is an equally renowned but cheaper red from the same area. Whites from Korčula, in particular **Pošip Čara**, are deliciously dry and golden.

Wine is either red (*crno*), white (*bijelo*) or, rarely, rosé (*crveno*), and dry (*suho*) or sweet (*slatko*). *Bevanda* is a (usually red) spritzer.

Beer is sold draught (*točeno*) or by the bottle, usually a local lager (Ožujsko, Karlovačko, sometimes Slovene Laško).

Clear, flavoured brandy (*rakija*) is the standard spirit, the grape variety (*loza*) sold everywhere. Other popular versions include *tvararica*, made with herbs, and *orahovača*, made with walnuts.

Coffee (*kava*) is strong and of decent quality. Sugar and milk are served in the saucer. *Kava sa mlijekom*, with milk, is quite milky. If you would like a standard cup with a dash of boiled milk, ask for a *veliki macchiato*. Tea (*čaj*) is either black or of the fruit variety.

Cafés & bars

The Old Town is full of drinking places. They start around 9am, when the terraces surrounding the focal square of Luža begin to fill. Most offer breakfast, snacks and brunches. The **graDskavana** is the best meeting place, **Café Cele** has the best cakes, **Dubrava**

the best sandwiches. Further down Stradun, the **Festival Café** offers more elaborate treats – at a price. If you're after a takeaway for the beach, **fresh*** sells wraps and smoothies; the Dubrovački kantun does decent sandwiches in summer.

Drinking also begins in the early hours – but you'll rarely see locals behaving disorderly. The best hubs for bars are up **Zamanjina** and **Vetranićeva**, and on **Bunićeva poljana**. Here, by the Cathedral, is the famous **Troubadour**, along with **Poco Loco**, **Mirage** and others, handy boltholes for when the sheer number of tourists becomes uncomfortable. Better still, dive behind the Jesuit Church and find one of the two cliff-face bars facing the sea, **Buža I** and **Buža II**. Old Town bars must close at 1am except during the **Dubrovnik Festival** in July and August.

In **Lapad** you'll find local bars lined on **Bana Josipa Jelačića** (including the rather splendid **Roxy**), on certain stretches of **Iva Vojnovića** and all the way down **šetalište kralja Zvonimira** as far as the beach. Spots in **Pile** include the Tovjerna Sesame, its front half a fine place to start or end the day. **La Bohème** nearby does cocktails but you'd be foolish not to venture further. The recently opened **Spice Lounge** at the Hotel Bellevue or, best of all, the **Sunset Lounge** at the Hotel Dubrovnik Palace, offer decent Martinis and a sea view you'll come back for.

Elsewhere, be aware that for local barmen, cocktail making is a circus act. Glass spinning and posing take priority over minor considerations such as mixing imaginative ingredients.

The main bar hub outside town is **Župa Dubrovačka**, a riviera of nightspots packed with locals in summer. **Srebreno** is the place to be, especially **Club 22** and **Porto**.

Algoritam

Shopping

No one comes to Dubrovnik for the shopping, though most are happy to browse the shopfronts on and off Stradun and the morning market on Gundulićeva poljana. The nearest supermarket is a modest one just beyond the Pile Gate or the large Konzum store by the ferry terminal in Gruž.

In the Old Town, no store is more than the size of a local post office, a frustrating limitation for ambitious boutique owners who are looking to shake things up a bit – such as urban style specialist Sheriff & Cherry, just in from Rovinj. Rents are astronomical and getting worse. Most downtown businesses, therefore, offer the easy options of souvenirs, postcards and foreign newspapers. You'll also find books,

CDs, cosmetics, hats, summer clothes, jewellery, domestic wines and olive oils, chocolates and the local speciality of ties and cravats. If you need something useful, like shoelaces or fluid for contact lenses, you'll probably have to leave the Old Town to get it.

To see how Dubrovnik looked before mass tourism came along, have a wander down Od Puča, lined with barber shops and fabric stores.

The lack of everyday shops can give the Old Town a feeling of being a tourist attraction rather than a living city. Nobody comes whistling out of their local grocer's any more. Big international chains, particularly design and fashion stores, are starting to move in too, and older locals are selling up.

Opening hours

Opening times vary enormously from shop to shop. Most open at 9am, some earlier, and close by about 7pm, often with a long lunch break. In high season, you can expect stores to stay open until 8pm or even later. Most close on Saturday afternoons, and few stay open on Sundays. The majority now open year-round, and close only for the main public holidays.

Payment

All outlets take local kuna in cash, and nearly all accept the major credit cards. Such is the prevalence of cruise-ship passengers passing through for a couple of hours, many places also take euros. Few market stallholders haggle – the older ones won't speak much English anyway – but if you're buying a bulk lot or the last of that day's goods, you could offer a simple sum in kuna.

Gifts & souvenirs

A phalanx of souvenir shops down Stradun sell pretty shoddy items: mugs, T-shirts, sunglasses, dolls, vases – anything with Dubrovnik written on it, in short.

Thankfully, sassier gifts do exist, and there are places where you can pick up presents you'd be happy to give and to receive.

The discerning shopper's first port of call should be Dubrovačka kuća, near the Ploče Gate. Whether you want cheap and cheerful or pricy and posh, the variety of goods is impressive: local wines and liquors, sweets and cakes, art books and posters. All are good quality. But the real jewel here is the Museum Shop. A long-term collaboration with the Museum of Arts and Crafts in Zagreb, it offers a floor full of great ceramics, crockery and glassware, all at pleasantly affordable prices.

S H O R T L I S T

Best fashion boutiques
- Croata (p73)
- jegerStar (p76)
- Kadena (p76)
- Ronchi (p77)
- Sheriff & Cherry (p77)

Best comestibles
- Dubrovačka kuća (p74)
- Franja Coffee & Teahouse (p74)
- Gruž market (p105)
- Gundulićeva poljana market (p74)
- Konzum (p105)
- Kraš Bonbonnière (p76)
- Vinoteka Dubrovnik (p77)

Best jewellery
- Djardin (p74)
- Eminence Art Workshop (p74)
- Ivana Bačura (p74)
- Trinity (p77)

Best art, crafts and souvenirs
- Art Studio Trabakul (p73)
- Artur Gallery (p78)
- DEŠA (p88)
- Dubrovačka kuća (p74)
- Galerija Sebastian (p80)
- Lapad market (p119)

Best for wine and spirits
- Dubrovačka kuća (p74)
- Vinoteka Dubrovnik (p77)
- Gundulićeva poljana market (p74)

Best for books and CDs
- Algebra bookshop (p72)
- Algoritam (p72)
- Aquarius (p73)

Best cosmetics
- Franciscan Monastery Pharmacy (p74)
- Lush (p77)

Best for kids
- Kraš Bonbonnière (p76)
- Turbo limač (p77)

The nearby Eminence Art Workshop is run by Emin, who makes and sells carvings – priced from 150kn to 4,000kn – from behind a battered desk. He also stocks work by Zvonimir Keček, who has a colourful, modern take on iconography.

Fashion & accessories

For a town in which locals like to dress to impress, there is a puzzling absence of good clothes shops. For the more streetwise, matters have improved with the opening of Sheriff & Cherry, with its finger on the urban pulse. There is also the more established and mainstream jegerStar. A significant number of visitors to Dubrovnik, however, aren't looking for hip – they just want something decent to wear.

At least women have Kadena, near the Pile Gate. It's a small, friendly shop stocking domestic designers' wares; mainly clothes,

but with some jewellery and accessories. One label that's worth looking at is Nebo, with its distinctive '60s style; Dado Zorica's jewellery is also a find.

Indeed, Dubrovnik has a number of jewellery stores. For necklaces, go to Trinity, with its three floors of bright coral, jade and pearls. It's a cut above its competitors – with prices to match. For sheer quantity, meanwhile, there's always Djardin. Ivana Bačura's studio produces contemporary, handmade pieces – stylish, simple and silver, with an original use of stones.

Food & drink

For everyday needs, head to the daily market near the main square. If you're taking a boat from Gruž that day, there's a bigger, cheaper market there too. Local produce, much of it from the nearby Konavle region, is sold until early afternoon. As well as picnic essentials, you'll find lavender oil from Hvar, olive oils and, if you ask carefully, local firewaters loza and travarica.

For the latter, more fancily packaged and considerably pricier, head for Vinoteka Dubrovnik on Stradun. Locals will flavour clear brandy with almost anything – look out for mistletoe, walnut or honey varieties. Vinoteka is where you'll find the best Croatian wines, from a robust, hearty red Dingač Barrique from nearby Pelješac to a golden yellow Pošip Čara from Korčula – perfect gifts. If you just want a standard bottle to take to the beach, stride out of the Pile Gate to the little grocer's on the right, and spend the money you'll save on cheeses and cold meats from the deli counter.

For a chocolatey treat, the best place to go is Kraš Bonbonnière, with an outlet on Stradun. Take home a box of Bajadera; irresistible sweet, nutty bricks.

Gruž market

Latino Club Fuego

WHAT'S BEST
Nightlife

For one of the busiest resorts in the Mediterranean, Dubrovnik hides its nightlife under a bushel. 'It's all folksy violins,' complains Andro Vidak, the prime mover and main promoter of DJ nights in and around Dubrovnik. 'The city council don't want to deal with popular culture at all.'

The most many people see of late entertainment is in the Old Town. After dark the narrow streets of Vetranićeva, Zamanjina, Dropćeva and, nearer Pile, Antuninska throng outside the destination bars of Africa, Casablanca and Talir. Casablanca plays the best music and should have a few flyers knocking about. All the bars in the Old Town have to close at 1am (except during Dubrovnik Festival

time when it's 3am). They're either unbearably packed in July or dead as a dodo in January.

The only nightclub option within the Old Town walls is Labirint, as uncomfortably snazzy as its restaurant. Venues outside the Old Town are not confined by the opening-hour restrictions imposed in the historic centre. Thus better options stand immediately through the gates bookending the Old Town. Lazareti, by the city beach in Ploče, is where to head if you want to be guaranteed quality late hours in central Dubrovnik. A multidisciplinary arts complex in a seafront quarantine barracks, Lazareti hosts the best local DJs and some international ones too. Also by the beach, East-West can be fun if you're dressed up for cocktails. The nearby Revelin Fort is lively but few people there will be over 25. Similarly, at the opposite end of the Old Town, through the Pile Gate, the Latino Club Fuego underpins a youthful, mainstream scene incorporating the nearby Capitano disco-bar.

Tips and rules

Admission fees are nominal. Unless it's for a big name DJ at a festival or special party at the Lazareti, the most you'll pay to get in is 50kn. Drinks prices are standard, slightly above what you'd pay at a local bar. The only places with a dress code are Labirint and East-West, where the rule is to be a bit smarter.

There'll be people on the door, but not barking inanely into earpiece microphones while frisking you. Drugs are in little evidence. The standard of DJing is generally good, although nothing as good as you would find around Croatia's real DJ hubs of Vodice, Zadar and Primošten, all in northern Dalmatia.

The live music scene is equally limited. Away from jazz nights packed with tourists outside the Troubador, the only interesting stuff will be found at Lazareti or the Orlando Klub, a grunge hangout in old hospital grounds halfway to the Lapad junction from the Pile Gate. DJ nights are also programmed there regularly.

Names to look out for are Tino, Gunč, Kaio and Lane, regular spinners at the Lazareti. A minimal style of techno is the preferred style of music. Look out for recently popular turbofolk – and avoid it. This simple, mindless pumping dance music with vague Balkan roots, practised by scantily-clad bimbos and boasting gangstas, has swept the nation. You'll know it when you hear it.

S H O R T L I S T

Best one-off venues
- Hotel Belvedere (p90)

Best for live music
- Lazareti (p90)
- Orlando Klub (p99)

Best mainstream discos
- Exodus (p121)
- Latino Club Fuego (p99)
- Revelin Club (p90)
- Vertigo (p24)

Liveliest Old-Town bars
- Africa (p59)
- Buža I (p60)
- Buža II (p61)
- Casablanca (p61)
- Galerie (p64)
- Ludwig (p67)
- Talir (p71)

Liveliest bars near the Old Town
- Capitano (p99)
- Laura (p87)
- Roxy (p117)

Liveliest spots in Lapad
- Casa Bar (p111)
- Orka (p114)

Best for jazz
- Orlandinjo Club (p121)
- Troubador (p71)

Best for cocktails
- Hemingway Bar (p64)
- Spice Lounge (p117)
- Sunset Lounge (p118)

Best morning-after bar
- Mališ (p102)

Best DJ destinations around Dalmatia
- Aurora, near Šibenik (p24)
- Barbarella's, near Zadar (p24)
- The Garden, Zadar (p24)
- Hacienda, Vodice (p24)
- Hawaii Beach, Orašac (p24)
- Porat, near Pirovac (p24)
- Veliki Žali, Brsečine (p24)

DON'T MISS

Alternative and way-out

Except for Lazareti and Orlando, finding anything alternative can be hard work. Mainstream discos, best exampled by Exodus in Lapad, dominate summer entertainment around the resort beaches. The best source, local-language only, is Andro Vidak's www.clubpages.net. The dates and DJ names are easy to work out but any information about individual venues is minimal.

One name to look out for though is the Hotel Belvedere. Erected as a prestigious congress hotel in the 1980s, bombed out by 1991, it overlooks everyone's favourite beach in Dubrovnik, Sveti Jakov. With the Old Town glittering in the background, DJs spin amid a ruined amphitheatre and cascades. Three key DJ nights were organised there in 2006, two with Ian Pooley, one with local radio Laus. Four more are promised for July and August 2007 – don't miss if you're in town.

Further down the coast is the resort of Župa Dubrovačka. In summer, locals flock here to party at Club 22, Porto and, in particular, Vertigo. These are all in Srebreno, a short drive from Dubrovnik.

North of town the scene is in flux after both Hawaii Beach at Orašac and particularly Veliki Žali at Brsečine near Trsteno underwent organisational problems in the winter of 2006. Keep an eye out in clubpages.net for any further developments. And if you're going up the coast beyond Split, the Hacienda (www.hacienda.hr) at Vodice and Aurora near Šibenik (www.auroraclub.hr) are serious clubbing landmarks all summer. Porat is the alternative version, 2km (1.25 miles) out of Pirovac on the coast road towards Zadar. Look out for glowing olive trees and you know you're there.

Further north, Zadar has become popular thanks to the arrival of Nick Colgan, a member of UB40's production crew. His landmark Garden (www.thegardenzadar.com) and Barbarella's, due to open in summer 2007, have put Zadar on the global clubbing map. A three-day DJ festival (www.thegarden festival2007.com) there from July 6 will be the best in the region.

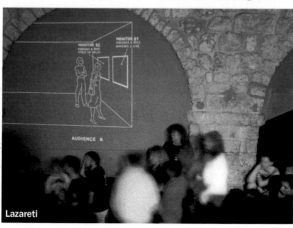

Lazareti

Carnival p26

WHAT'S BEST
Arts & Leisure

Dubrovnik is obviously not short of culture. The birthplace of revered playwrights, baroque poets and celebrated artists of the Dubrovnik School, the town hosts one of Europe's most established and revered arts events, the seven-week long **Dubrovnik Festival**. Set in historic, atmospheric venues in and around the Old Town, some outdoors, the festival focuses firmly on traditional and highbrow genres. Impromptu street entertainment and late bar hours keep the casual visitor interested.

Dubrovnik's other main annual cultural event takes place shortly before this and always attracts a foxier crowd, both in terms of audience and celebrities: the **Libertas Film Festival**.

The other 44 weeks of the year, you have to search high and low for cultural impetus. There is one theatre, the **Marin Drzić**, whose programme is centred on the literary heritage of Dubrovnik. The MD also accommodates the odd chamber concert and *klapa* show, traditional local a cappella singing, dull as ditchwater. There is one cinema, the **Sloboda** – a couple of other open-air ones are set up in summer. Equipment and seating are quite wonderfully antiquated – at the door they hand out cushions to prevent sore backsides. There are two main venues where modern live music is regularly played, both places better known for being putting on DJs: **Lazareti** and the **Orlando Klub**.

Copacabana beach

There are two decent contemporary galleries, the **Museum of Modern Art** and the **Dulčić, Masle and Pulitika**; and two photography galleries worthy of mention – the **Carmel Photo Gallery** and **War Photo Limited**.

So you'll find no contemporary dance, precious little contemporary theatre (look out for what the **Lero** puts on twice a year), no comedy, no gay scene to speak of and little arthouse cinema. The **Dubrovnik Symphony Orchestra** has been playing since 1924, first as the Dubrovnik City Orchestra, then as the Dubrovnik Festival Orchestra – they perform standards at the Revelin Fort. There is, in short, little to dress up or dress down for.

The only exceptions are the town's carnival and public celebrations that brighten an otherwise moribund calendar.

Taking it to the streets

Dubrovnik excels in traditional ceremony and procession, both religious and secular. The main one is the procession for the **Festival of St Blaise**. Taking place every February 3, this celebration of Dubrovnik's patron saint is yet another incantation of the glory of the past. The baldachins of brocade and the gold of the saint's relics, the parish flags and sumptuous traditional costumes combine to offer annual thanksgiving for protection and prosperity.

Immediately afterwards begins the **carnival** or *poklade*. Although it can't be compared to the riches seen in Venice, Dubrovnik's carnival is more spontaneous. The few locals who go to work do so in masks, and the whole event ends in a big party at the Revelin Fort.

Art for all

The one trump card Dubrovnik has up its sleeve is art. What is of most interest relates to the 15th, late 19th and early 20th centuries.

Although much was lost in the 1667 earthquake, the few surviving works by the craftsmen of the Dubrovnik School show something of an artistic tradition passed down from father to son, and in a system of apprenticeships. Italian influence shows throughout. In the case of its most celebrated exponent, **Nikola Božidarević**, the style shows more local character, possibly because of the number of renowned Ragusan artists this early 16th-century painter worked under. To see something of his art, head out of the Old Town through the Pile Gate, past Gradac Park and down Od Graca, to the little votive church of **Our Lady of Danče**. Housed inside is the artist's last work, a triptych image of the Virgin Mary and two saints, one of whom displays a portrait of the artist reflected in one of his swords. Works by other great names from the period – **Lovro Dobričević**, **Mihajlo Hamzić** – can be found in the **Dominican Monastery**.

There you will also find *The Miracle of St Dominic*, one of more than 2,000 works by the most celebrated local artist of the modern era, **Vlaho Bukovac**. Born in Cavtat in 1855, and Italian by birth, Bukovac moved to Paris where he studied at the Ecole des Beaux-Arts. He was the first Croatian member of the Paris Salon. His work, mainly portraits with no few landscapes, is influenced by Impressionism yet tempered by academism. He made good use of pointillist brush strokes, creating a kind of sweet realism, bright and colourful. His works are displayed in the Museum of Modern Art, and Dulčić, Masle and Pulitika Gallery. If you get a hankering to see more, his house and gallery are at Cavtat, 15km away, reached by regular bus or by boat from the old harbour.

Sport & leisure

The spectator sport that stirs the local imagination is **water polo**. Not that there's a great public arena – the action is on Dubrovnik's beaches between teams of each

SHORTLIST

Most anticipated events
- Carnival (p26)
- Festival of St Blaise (p26)

Best art festivals
- Dubrovnik Festival (p30)
- Libertas Film Festival (p32)

Best cinemas
- Jadran cinema (p80)
- Lapad cinema (p121)
- Sloboda cinema (p80)

Best theatre
- Marin Držić Theatre (p80)

Best spectator sports
- Divlja Liga water polo (p120)

Best activity clubs
- Adriatic Kayak Tours (p99)
- Adriatic Sea Kayaking (p121)
- Adventure Dalmatia (p99)
- Blue Planet Diving (p121)
- Navis Underwater Explorers (p121)

Best venues for temporary exhibitions
- Artur Gallery (p78)
- Museum of Modern Art (p84)

DON'T MISS

beach. The so-called **Divlja Liga**, 'Wild League', takes place in July and August, with the grand final at the old harbour.

Local football club **NK GOŠK Dubrovnik** recently made the second division. They play at a modest ground in Lapad, at kralja Tomislava and Ispod Petke. Bars in Gruž (where they were formed) and Lapad display their pennants.

Most top hotels have pools, gyms and saunas. Some in Lapad share tennis courts too. You'll also find **diving schools**, and clubs that offer **sea kayaking** for beginners. The best of these is **Adriatic Kayak Tours**, who also include white-water rafting, hiking and mountain biking on their agenda.

You have chosen
the best destination …
Now choose
the best quality
mobile network!

You're visiting Croatia. Relax. Feel as if you're at home, with Vip roaming services.

Tourist info - call 7799 and get information about destinations, accomodation, events and other travel information in Croatia.

Tourist guide - find a site that interests you, call 7766 and discover everything you want to know about cultural heritage of Croatia.

Prepaid Roaming Top-up for Vodafone subscribers - as a Vodafone prepaid user you can top-up your account by buying Vipme prepaid vouchers, anywhere in Croatia. This service is valid only for customers of certain Vodafone networks.

Home Short Code Services - access your voicemail or call your home customer service by dialing the same short numbers that you do in your own country.

For further information visit www.vipnet.hr

Calendar

Dubrovnik Summer Festival p31

Dubrovnik is best known for its annual **Summer Festival**. The most important arts event in the region, this well-established showcase for (mainly) theatre, classical music and dance has two characteristics: the quality of its high-brow programme and the magical nature of its venues. Much takes place outdoors, around the Old Town, or within the walls of grand, historic sights such as the Revelin Fort or Lovrijenac fortress.

Not only does this seven-week festival dominate the summer season – impromptu performances take place around the Old Town, and rooms in the better hotels fill up fast – it also overshadows the cultural agenda throughout the year. The only other major annual arts event is the **Libertas Film Festival**, which has had to raise its profile to compete with the **Dubrovnik International Film Festival** and invite big-name international guests to town. Meanwhile, the future of the DIFF is unclear.

Libertas has had to reschedule around the Dubrovnik Festival, to a slot a fortnight earlier. This also ensures that it doesn't clash with the nearby **Sarajevo Film Festival** (www.sff.ba) in late August, a real biggie.

Dubrovnik also likes to dress up for the big occasion, for traditional public celebrations and processions – **Christmas**, **New Year**, the **Festival of St Blaise** and, most of all, the four-day **carnival** every February. Although not as big as the one in Venice, it's just as traditional, dating from the 14th century, and is more spontaneous.

Dubrovnik Summer Festival

Approaching its 60th anniversary, the **Dubrovnik Summer Festival** (Dubrovačke ljetne igre) is one of Europe's most established celebrations of the classical arts.

For 47 days and nights, from July 10 to August 25, the streets, churches, squares and famous buildings of the Old Town host the big names in classical music, theatre, opera and dance. Shows bring Dubrovnik's historic jewels to life. Shakespeare is performed open-air at the Lovrijenac fortress, orchestras play at the Sponza Palace, piano soloists at the Cathedral, ballet takes place after dark outside St Blaise's Church and all kinds of events have the moonlit City Walls as a backdrop. Some 70 venues are used – even Lokrum island. In 2006, 2,000 artists came from 20 countries to perform 31 plays, 33 concerts, nine folk shows and one ballet.

The festival has taken place every year since 1950. In the war of 1992, in place of an opening ceremony, locals lit candles in the windows while Ivan Gundulić's *Anthem to Freedom* played on the radio to a deserted Stradun.

In peacetime, the festival has expanded its schedule and its scope, inviting big names; Derek Jacobi and Daniel Day Lewis have appeared as Hamlet, a festival mainstay. The core programme remains the classical arts but modernity has widened the remit. Experimental works, puppet theatre, and contemporary writers now share the stage with local heavyweight playwright Marin Držić, Goethe, Molière and the Greek tragedies.

Confirmed highlights for 2007 include composer Krzysztof Penderecki conducting the Sinfionetta Cracovia, the Paris Opera Ballet and the CityDance Ensemble from Washington.

Book ahead (www.dubrovnik-festival.hr) for the biggest events – for others you can pay on the door. There will also be book launches, art exhibitions and other dos that have sprung up to take advantage of the increased number of visitors in town. Hotels and restaurants fill – book early in all cases. For the most prestigious events, smart dress, although not obligatory, is expected.

The following are the pick of the annual events in Dubrovnik. More details and dates can be found in the free monthly *Dubrovnik Guide* at tourist offices. Dates highlighted in **bold** are public holidays. *See also* www.tzdubrovnik.com.

January

1 Jan **Nova Godina (New Year's Day)**
The Dubrovnik Symphony Orchestra plays a traditional New Year concert in the Church of St Blaise. The repertoire is crowd-pleasing: waltzes, polkas, opera hits and classic melodies. The event takes place during the during the first week of January, as often as possible on New Year's Day itself.

6 Jan **Bogojavljenje (Epiphany)**
This national holiday sees families gather after mass and the Christmas decorations taken down around town.

February

2-3 Feb 2008 **Festival of St Blaise**
One of the biggest events of the year is the honouring of the patron saint of Dubrovnik. The celebration is marked by a traditional procession of colourful flags, shining gold, brocade and bright costumes, the saint's relics are carried through the Old Town, before mass. By the evening, street entertainment breaks out and locals congregate in the main squares for communal drinking and dancing.

11-16 Feb 2008 **Karnivo (Dubrovnik Carnival)**
The best time to visit in winter is for the annual carnival, the *poklade* or *karnivo*. Brass bands, colourful parades and masked balls are the main features of the week-long celebration. Even people having to work on these days go to the office wearing masks. Celebrations end with a big party at the Revelin Fort.

March

16 Mar 2008/5 Apr 2009
Cvjetnica (Palm Sunday)
Celebrations take place at churches in the Old Town. Children take in olive twigs to be blessed. A big build-up during the week leading up to Easter sees processions on various Dalmatian islands, including Korčula.

23 Mar 2008/**12** Apr 2009
Uskrs (Easter Sunday)
Busy morning mass at churches around the Old Town.

24 Mar 2008/**13** Apr 2009
Uskršnji ponedjeljak (Easter Monday)
Families meet and greet – holiday atmosphere around town.

May

1 May 2008 **Medjunarodni praznik rada (May Day)**
National public holiday.

22 May 2008/**11** June 2009
Tijelovo (Corpus Christi)
Religious holiday 60 days after Easter.

June

22 June 2008 **Dan antifašičke borbe (Anti-fascist Struggle Day)**
A national holiday to commemorate the Sisak partisans who founded their unit on this day in 1941.

25 June 2008 **Dan državnosti (Statehood Day)**
Marks the day in 1991 when Croatia declared its independence from Yugoslavia, at the same time as Slovenia – not to be confused with Independence Day on October 8.

29 June-4 July 2007 **Libertas Film Festival**
www.libertasfilmfestival.com
This week-long celebration of celluloid brings the stars to town. See box p32.

July

10 July-25 Aug 2007/10 July - 25 Aug 2008 **Dubrovačke ljetne igre (Dubrovnik Summer Festival)**
www.dubrovnik-festival.hr
The biggest bash of the year is this seven-week long major arts event at 70 venues around the Old Town. Book your hotel room early. See box p30.

DON'T MISS

Libertas Film Festival

Open-air films, sun, sea and Old Town locations – the fledging contemporary week-long **Libertas Film Festival** (p31) has a lot going for it. In a balance of mainstream movies, the less obscure arthouse features, documentaries and the latest achievements of Croatian film industry, Libertas 2006 showed Robert Altman and Terry Gilliam.

Libertas made its debut in 2005, with the Croatian première of sci-fi drama *Nochnoi Dozor* (the 'Russian Matrix') by Timur Bekmambetov. The Dubrovnik International Film Festival (DIFF) had already been established in 2003. Each event competed for global profile. The DIFF brought over Christopher Walken; Libertas invited Owen Wilson and Woody Harrelson.

There's been a battle of schedules too. Libertas is now booked for June 29 2007; DIFF 2006 passed by somewhat unnoticed in October 2006. It is not sure where DIFF is going next. Neither can clash with the gargantuan **Dubrovnik Summer Festival**, which gets all the attention for nearly two months of the peak season.

Libertas venues include the **Sloboda** cinema (p80), site of the festival office, the **Marin Držić Theatre** (p80) and the **Revelin Fort** (p84). Tickets go on sale at the Sloboda an hour before each performance, all at affordable prices.

The full programme for 2007 will be confirmed in May – check the website for details.

August

5 Aug Dan pobjede i domovinske zahvalnosti (Victory and Homeland Thanksgiving Day)
This public holiday marks the crucial liberation of Knin in 1995 that turned the Yugoslav war in Croatia's favour.

15 Aug Velika Gospa (Feast of the Assumption)
Religious holiday in Croatia.

September

1-18 Sept Dubrovnik-Biograd Fun Rally
www.sunsail.com/au
This regatta takes in the entire Dalmatian coast on its journey between Dubrovnik and Biograd.

October

8 Oct Dan nezavisnosti (Independence Day)
This national holiday marks the day in 1991 when the Croatian parliament cut all ties with Yugoslavia.

November

1 Nov Dan svih svetih (All Saints' Day)
Candles are lit and placed in churches and at cemeteries around Dubrovnik.

December

24/25 Dec Božić (Christmas)
Family meals (fish, often cod, not meat) take place on Christmas Eve, *Badnjak*, when the Christmas table is arranged. *Badnji kruh*, traditional bread made with honey, nuts and dried fruit, is also prepared. The main meal (suckling pig, turkey) is served on the 25th – presents are given on either day. Carol singing takes place around the Old Town. Churches open their doors at midnight.

26 Dec Sveti Stjepan (St Stephen's Day/Boxing Day)
More family feasting.

31 Dec New Year's Eve
Local dignitaries greet the crowds on Stradun, bars and restaurants fill out. Celebrations are organised at the town's major hotels.

Itineraries

Round the City Walls

The easiest and most popular itinerary for visitors to Dubrovnik is the stroll around its fortifications. It also should be the first, as it allows the newcomer to get their bearings, plus it offers an appreciation of the scale of this intricate jewel, the skill of those who designed and constructed it – and some breathing space from the high-season masses below. It's an elevated promenade and history lesson in one.

As you arrive in the Old Town through the **Pile Gate**, the main entrance and ticket office is immediately on your left – although you can also start (and finish) your walking tour from signposted openings at the other end of the

Old Town, near the **Aquarium** and the **Revelin Fort**, both either side of the old harbour.

You can set your own pace, take an hour or an afternoon. Audio-guides (30kn) in English are sold at the main entrance but most visitors are perfectly content with random vistas of red tiled roofs or, better still, the panoramic blue of the Adriatic, interspersed with pristine white stones jutting into it down below from varying angles. In high season, pedestrian jams can build up. Nearly all sections are lined with walls at least waist-, if not chest-high, so anyone nervous about heights needn't fret. A couple of cafés provide perfect pit stops at the harbour end, where there's also an open terrace for that eye-popping backdrop, ideal for holiday snaps.

Dubrovnik's fortifications are 1,940 metres long. The sea-facing ones are between 1.5 metres and three metres thick, those set towards **Mount Srdj** between four and six metres. They are interspersed by four prominent forts, **Minčeta**, **Sv Luka**, **Sv Ivan** and **Bokar**, five bastions, 12 square towers, and protected by two great fortresses, Revelin in the north-east corner and **Lovrijenac** down in the south-east. Along the northern and eastern flanks, to guard against attack from the hills, a ditch some 17 metres wide made the Old Town practically inaccessible to any invader.

This, the mother of all medieval fortifications, was the symbol of Dubrovnik's power and guile. No palace or sumptuous edifice would have suited the Ragusa Republic, a state that banned slavery in 1416. There was a public home for old people. Education was paramount. That century, Onofrio's Great Fountain, still standing inside the Pile Gate, provided a regular supply of clean water to the city. The Senate was elected every year, the ruling Rector every month. Of its day, these City Walls contained one of the most advanced, well-organised and forward-thinking societies in Europe.

Work on a wall around the city began sometime in the 13th century, advancing after a great fire in town in 1296. Wood was never used again. The decision in the 14th century to erect sturdy fortifications, as Ragusa began to compete with Venice, literally set in stone the compact size of the Old Town you see today. To walk down the main bisecting thoroughfare of **Stradun** between the Gates of Pile and **Ploče** only takes ten minutes, 15 if it's crowded.

Ragusa's most feared enemies were the Venetians – and the Turks. Once Constantinople fell to the Ottomans in 1453, alarm bells rang in Ragusa. By 1461 the city fathers had hired the services of the renowned Florentine master **Michelozzo di Bartolomeo Michelozzi**, designer of the Medici Palace. Michelozzo only stayed a couple of years, in which he bickered with the Senate over his timesheet and blueprints, but during that time he gave the City Walls the cylindrical look still apparent more than 500 years later. The Bokar Tower is his. Michelozzo also began to shape the graceful yet impregnable Minčeta Tower, integral to the walls as a whole. Before heading back to Florence in a huff, Michelozzo left plans for others to follow. **Juraj Dalmatinac** of Zadar continued where Michelozzo had left off, working both on Minčeta and the Revelin Fort.

After Dalmatinac – said to have fled to escape an outbreak of plague – local architect **Paškoje Milićević** stepped in to complete the job over five decades into the 16th century. Milićević built the bridges leading from the Pile and Ploče Gates into the Old Town. He was also responsible for the fortifications around the old harbour, so great was the fear of attack by sea. Around the walls, little openings allowed locals to throw their rubbish into the sea and officials to carry out regular, meticulous inspections of the craftsmen's work, stone by stone. Nothing was left to chance. When the terrible earthquake levelled much of the Old Town in 1667, the walls stayed firm. Indeed, surviving members of the Senate congregated in an intact Revelin Fort to restore social order and devise plans for Dubrovnik's rapid reconstruction.

ITINERARIES

As you walk under the Pile Gate, heading for the tour entrance, you notice the statue of St Blaise, patron saint and protector of Dubrovnik, who oversaw the deliberate dying out of the noble line here, once Napoleon's troops and the Habsburgs took over.

Climbing past the entrance, walkers have a choice of heading clockwise, straight for the nearby Minčeta Tower, the highest of the vantage points – or heading anti-clockwise, past the smaller towers of **Gornji ugao** and **Sv Frane** (burned following the 1667 earthquake), over the Pile Gate and towards Bokar. This section was completed in its entirety over ten years in the 1450s. In the distance stretches Boninovo and sleek, white Jadrolinija ships at the port of Gruž.

Michelozzo's masterpiece of Bokar took a century to complete, overseen by Antonio Ferramolino. Cannons once stood on the terrace; it's now one of many aerial stages for the **Dubrovnik Festival**. Immediately opposite is the free-standing fort of Lovrijenac, another open-air theatre come festival time, known in particular for performances of *Hamlet*. Standing 37 metres above the sea, proudly emblazoned with the motto '*Non bene pro toto libertas venditur auro*' ('Liberty is not for sale, not even for gold'), Lovrijenac contains its own history. A fortified look-out post was placed here as long ago as the early 11th century. Rebuilt 300 years later, it was reinforced by Dalmatinac in the mid 1400s, after the fall of Constantinople. Soldiers stood guard here round the clock – there was also a kitchen and tank for rainwater. The fortifications and the watch quickly increased when news filtered through of the imminent arrival of the great Battle of Lepanto of 1571. Crucially, the Ottoman forces were defeated.

Following damage in the 1667 earthquake, and no longer able to support heavy cannons, Lovrijenac was reconstructed according to designs by **Miho Hranjac**, with a series of terraces. After the fall of Ragusa, the cannons were taken away by the French and Austrians, most were melted down for weaponry. A handful are still on display in the Museum of Military History in Vienna. Under the Habsburgs, the fort became a prison then, either side of World War I, a hotel. In World War II, the Italian forces reconverted it into a prison. After the war it was renovated to provide a stage for summer theatre.

Walking along the south wall, washing hangs out in the small squares of courtyard gardens and to your left, you can peek over into people's living-rooms. You pass the bastions of Miličević's **Mrtvo zvono** (the 'Dead Bell', otherwise known as **Sv Petar**), **Zvijezda** (still ruined today from 1667), **Sv Margarita** and **Sv Stjepan**. Here stands an inviting café – you're halfway round. Below, the waves lap against the rocks. On flat sections just above, pleasure seekers sunbathe, sip cocktails and dive into the Adriatic. This is **Buža**, the Hole in the Wall (p62) bar.

As you approach **Sv Spasitelj** on the south-east corner, the verdant island of **Lokrum** comes into full view. A short and regular hop from the old harbour, it looks wild and exotic, a haven for nudists and sun worshippers.

You now arrive at the old harbour, guarded by the twin forts of **Sv Ivan** and **Sv Luka**. Sv Ivan also guards the most secrets. It was once two towers – look at Nikola Božidarević's triptych *Our Lady with the Saints* in the Dominican Church and you'll see how it was in the early 16th century. By 1577

City Walls

Sv Ivan had been converted into a masterpiece of military architecture by Miličević. Today the building accommodates the twin attractions of the **Maritime Museum** and the **Aquarium**.

Above the harbour and adjoining **Arsenal**, past the main square of **Luža**, the **Rector's Palace** and the **Sponza Palace**, you pass Sv Luka and stand opposite the Revelin Fort. Formerly another administrative centre for the Senate, now a **discotheque**, it is another stage for the Dubrovnik Festival, with a view over the harbour. This was the most protected of the fortresses – here the annual tribute delivered to placate the Ottoman sultan was kept.

Over Ploče Gate, heading towards Minčeta, the north wall faces the hills from which Serbian gunners bombarded the city in 1991-92. High above stands Mount Srdj and the **Imperial Fort**. The old cablecar station here is still a ruin, frequently rumoured to be in line for renovation. However, the surrounding hillsides are still dotted with ordnance.

The stretch between the Ploče Gate and Minčeta was built in under three years, as soon as news came of the fall of Constantinople in 1453. Past the bastions of **Sv Jakov**, **Sv Katalina** and **Sv Barbara**, Minčeta was built to complex plans laid down by Michelozzo, who first failed to convince the Senate of his scheme. Dalmatinac completed the work, and the tower's elegant curved appearance. The stunning view of the walls, Old Town and sea is ample reward for an enjoyable morning's trek.

Portoč

Lokrum by Boat

Lokrum is for lovers and legends. This unspoilt island lush with pines, palms and cypress trees basks in the Adriatic less than a kilometre from the Old Town. Its verdant coastline beckons from the hotel windows of Ploče. Dotted with diverse ruins and remnants – medieval and ecclesiastical, Napoleonic, Habsburg – it has long been given over to nature.

After attempts by the Venetians, French and Austrians to conquer and build on it, before damage from the Serbian bombardment of 1991, Lokrum was a UNESCO-protected island nature reserve. No rubbish, no dogs, no fires, no smoking, no overnight stays.

Between April and October, the boat traffic from the mainland is constant. You can be drinking a beer in Dubrovnik's main square and be here within 20 minutes. Little open taxi-boats pour over from the old harbour every half-hour (35kn return) yet those arriving in the morning feel as if the whole island is theirs. A gecko, turtle or snake lizard might pop up. Buzzards, grey falcons and swifts nest here in any given spring or autumn. Man is free to frolic naked around Cape Skrinja, round the corner from Portoč, the jetty for the taxi boat. Lovers carve their names on the cactus leaves. In late summer, stunning fluorescent blue damselfish appear through seagrass brushed by starfish and sea urchins. A more idyllic part of the city – and Lokrum feels close enough to say, the Château d'If to Marseille – you could not imagine.

Yet mention Lokrum to an older local and you will hear tales of curses and ill fortune. The liveliest of these legends surrounds the departure of the Benedictine monks, settled on Lokrum since

1023, the invading French and the island's subsequent takeover by various ill-fated Habsburgs.

Up until then, Lokrum's only historical footnote was it having given shelter to Richard the Lionheart after being shipwrecked in 1192. So grateful was the lost Crusader, he swore he would build a votive church on the island. Persuaded to build one on the mainland instead, Richard's church (site of today's Cathedral, rebuilt on top of the one destroyed by the 1667 earthquake) became a matter of dispute between the monks and Ragusan authorities for centuries.

On the fateful eve of their departure in 1798, the monks tramped around Lokrum in candlelit procession. A curse is said to have resulted from their solemn farewell. A temporary stay then followed by the French – blamed by some parties for ordering the monks' departure. Soon afterwards, rich Ragusans who bought the island suffered various strokes of misfortune – but nothing like as bad as the Austrian nobility to whom they sold Lokrum, lock, stock and barrel, in 1859.

The buyer, Maximilian, brother of Austro-Hungarian Emperor Franz Josef, loved Lokrum. Much to local disapproval, he turned the island into his own pleasure garden, building the summer residence you can still see mingled with the ruins of the medieval monastery complex a short walk from Portoč. Around it were his exotic gardens. Some 150 years later, imported plants blend with native ones, such is the humid climate of the island. Maximilian's tree-lined walks run through the island; the Path of Paradise leads from the Napoleonic Fort Royal to his residence via an old olive grove planted by the Benedictines. Peacocks still roam here but not the

parrots Maximilian also brought. Near the ruined fort, by Skalica where Richard landed, is the Cross of Triton. It was built by Maximilian in honour of the sailors who died when the ship of the same name that had first brought him here mysteriously exploded when at anchor.

After three happy summers here, Maximilian and his beloved Belgian wife Charlotte were parted when Franz Josef dispatched his brother to Mexico to be emperor. His fate, shot by a firing squad, was famously painted by Manet. Back in Europe, Charlotte went completely mad. On her return to Lokrum, her yacht overturned and she was saved, again according to local legend, by coral hunters.

Subsequent Habsburgs who set foot on Lokrum suffered strange misfortunes: the heir Rudolf and his unexplained double suicide with his lover at Mayerling; and his mother, the empress Elisabeth, who was stabbed to death in a random act by an Italian anarchist at Lake Geneva. As if to underline the point, before his assassination in Sarajevo in June 1914, Franz Ferdinand was looking forward to a summer sojourn on Lokrum. The shot finished the dynasty for good.

The attraction of Lokrum for today's visitors remains. In its south-west corner, a lake of warm saltwater, the so-called Dead Sea, formed by tectonic fracture, is surrounded by rocky beaches. In the middle bloom botanical gardens beside a tranquil café-restaurant.

There is, of course, no hotel. The last boats leave for Dubrovnik around 7pm, depending on the time of year. Check if you're planning to spend a long day there. The service closes at the end of October and starts up again on the last day of March. Check information with Rezervat Lokrum (020 427 242).

ITINERARIES

Lokrum

Lapad by Bus

Dubrovnik doesn't do tour buses. Some of the snootier hotels might lay on something, but the **Old Town** is pedestrianised, the open square of **Brsalje** by the **Pile Gate** is traffic-choked and the road towards Gruž is often gridlocked. Anyone seeking a tour bus licence would be laughed out of town.

What is the more curious tourist to do? The answer is simple. Three times an hour, from 5.40am to past midnight, the **no.4 bus** deposits all incoming passengers, does a sharp U-turn just before the car-clogged Pile Gate to come to a brief halt by the Libertas ticket booth.

In its 20-minute journey from the Pile Gate to the very tip of **Lapad** and a stunning view of all the islands dotted around Dubrovnik, the trusty no.4 will pass a dozen of the city's key hotels, including the new boutique **Bellevue** and the yet-to-open high-end **Libertas**

Rixos. It can take you to hubs of nightlife away from the Old Town, to restaurants you would not have visited but perhaps should, Lapad beach, an open-air cinema and even Dubrovnik's only laundrette. Those going all the way will get a better handle on Dubrovnik, rather than a passing knowledge of shopfronts along Stradun in the Old Town.

The no.4 also offers scenery in spades. Sit on either side for sea views, to the left as you leave the Pile Gate, to the right as the no.4 motors along Masarykov put and its destination with a match-winning sunset. Buy your ticket (single 8kn, day pass 25kn) from the booth, pass it through the machine by the driver and hop on.

The bus will first rumble up the incline of Dr Ante Starčevića, leaving behind Pile and the grandiose façade of the **Hilton Hotel** to pass through **Boninovo**, a neighbourhood characterised by a rugged sea view on one side, and on the other, a cemetery, untended villas and an open-air cinema, the **Kino Slavica**. Although currently shut for renovation, the Slavica, with its panoramic bar terrace, is expected at the end of the 2007 season. Hidden amid the greenery and Italianate houses are cocktail bar **La Bohème** and the **Orlando Klub**, a live music and DJ spot.

The bus will then stop at a main junction. Two parallel roads lead to Gruž, towards the bus station and the harbour. Also parallel, to the left of Ante Starčevića, is Bana Josipa Jelačića. Walk up it for five minutes and you'll find a handy hub of bars: Ferrari, Boogie Woogie, Casanova and, most of all, the quite wonderful **Roxy**.

Our buses, though, veers left onto Lapad, Dubrovnik's verdant playground, area of the town's busiest beaches, liveliest stretches of bars and most tourist-friendly hotels. The main road to the leisure area is initially called Pera Čingrije. Almost immediately, the stunning new **Hotel Bellevue** comes into view. Opened in February 2007, it houses a panoramic pool, a high-end restaurant and cocktail bar, extravagantly designed, and cut into the cliff face of **Danče Bay**. The **Vapor** restaurant and **Spice Lounge** bar, and their elevated sea-view terraces, are open to the public. Budget-conscious travellers can stay at the **Hotel Lero** diagonally opposite – Dubrovnik's only launderette is next door.

As it cuts between the residential districts of Montovjerna, Gospino polje and Hladnica, Pera Čingrije becomes **Iva Vojnovića**. First on the left-hand side, then on the right, key nightspots for locals line the main road. Bars such as **Time Out**, **El Toro**, **Cohiba**, **Paradiso**, **Apollo**, **Petrunjela**, **Mirakul** and

XLNT pack out in summer, few tourists among the young clientele. On the other side quality mid-range restaurants include **Teatar** and **Belvedere**. A visitor gets the sense of Dubrovnik getting on with daily business away from the shop window of the Old Town. A row of stores and, further down, **Lapad Shopping Centre** and **market**, augment the sense of community.

Until this point, the no.4 bus has been sharing road space with the nos.2, 5, 6A and 7. At the next main junction, with **Ispod Petke**, the no.4 heads west towards the panoramic point of Rt Petka. Ispod Petke runs parallel to **Mata Vodopića** and **šetalište kralja Zvonimira**. The latter is the car-free street lined with bars, cafés and restaurants – **Aè**, **Konavoka**, **Van** – leading down to **Lapad beach**. To reach the bar-lined path, either use one of the other buses or get off at this junction and walk for ten minutes. To reach the beach, stay on the no.4, which will pass five mid-range resort hotels – **Komodor**, **Adriatic**, **Uvala**, **Vis** and **Splendid** – while skirting the south-west corner of the shorefront. In high season, you'll see the crowded seaside ahead. If you're just looking to reach the beach from the Old Town, it's the 11th stop from the Pile Gate.

Just past this point is where practicality ends and panoramic sightseeing takes over. Setting off at right angles to šetalište kralja Zvonimira near the Hotel Park, **Masarykov put** runs behind Lapad beach. Here, the no.4 joins it and runs with it, hugging close to the jagged coastline. Beyond, on the right-hand side, is nothing but pure blue. The splodges in the near distance are the rocky **Grebeni** islets – Kantenari, Vješala, Greben – whose only evidence of human habitation is a lighthouse on the

Lapad seafront

ITINERARIES

latter. Beyond Greben, to the north, stretches the better known and verdant Elafiti archipelago. Of its 13 islands, the three inhabited ones – **Koločep**, **Lopud** and **Šipan** – are key destinations in summer. Each contains at least one hotel should you wish to stay.

The far west coast of Šipan faces the tip of perhaps Croatia's most idyllic island, **Mljet**. Most of the thousands of visitors who take the ferry from Gruž to the ports of Sobra and Polače are heading for the western half of the island, its national park and lakes. The far eastern tip you see from Šipan can be a more attractive proposition, boasting the unspoiled, uncrowded sandy beaches of **Saplunara**.

Back on the mainland, the no.4 trundles on to its destination. After one stop halfway along the coast, the bus cuts through swathes of tree-lined landscape until it reaches its terminus, and deep in greenery, the swish façade of the upmarket **Hotel Dubrovnik Palace**.

Just as its original architect Vincek conceived it in 1972, the Dubrovnik Palace is set in a tangle of woodland paths, just before two forks of the south-west tip of Lapad. Damaged in the 1991

shelling, the Dubrovnik Palace was bought and completely overhauled by the Adriatic Luxury Hotels group. The result is a five-star wonder, winner of the Best Hotel in Croatia award at London's World Travel Market in 2005 and 2006. For non-guests, the attraction here is the **Sunset Lounge**, an upscale cocktail bar whose expanse extends the length of a stupendous view of sea, islands, slow boats in between, sky and, if you time your visit right, the sunset in question. Drinks here are set at standard prices for Dubrovnik, and include the finest Croatian wines and clear, flavoured brandies. Much is discounted during the late-afternoon happy hour. Cocktails, Manhattans, Mojitos and Daiquiris, are best enjoyed in the early evening, when a piano player sets up and lights beyond start to twinkle.

No need for a taxi back, not until midnight anyway. Awaiting you right outside the lobby, your trusty no.4 will whisk you back to the Old Town. You could even stop off for nightcaps at Lapad beach, Iva Vojnovića, Bana Josipa Jelačića, La Bohème or the **Latino Club Fuego**, right next to the in-bound Pile Gate terminus.

Lapad beach

Dubrovnik by Area

Stradun p58

Old Town

When locals are asked by other Croatians where they are from, they say simply: '*Grad*'. Short for Stari Grad, or Old Town, the retort reinforces the importance of the compact, historic centre in the psyche. Contained within the City Walls, bisected by the 292-metre long main street of **Stradun**, Stari Grad *is* Dubrovnik.

Many tourists come here and shuttle continuously between the gates at either end, **Pile** and **Ploče**. Stradun heaves in July and August – you'll want to escape. Boats run regularly from the **old harbour** to the nearby island of **Lokrum** or follow the signs for a panoramic beer, swimming and sunbathing at **Buža I** and **II**.

The closely packed side streets contain any number of bars and restaurants, many of the latter uninspiring. Most offer the same dishes, delivered in the same style. Recent exceptions – **Wanda**, the **Dubrovački kantun**, the short-lived **Sapur** – provide hope that more adventurous dining may one day become the rule. Except during **Dubrovnik Festival** time, bars must close at 1am. The nightspots outside Pile and Ploče Gates are all five minutes' walk away.

Although the Old Town boasts a **Cathedral**, the **Rector's Palace**, two monasteries, museums of pharmacy and sailing, a mosque, a synagogue, an Orthodox church and a dozen Catholic ones, the only must-do is to walk the **City Walls**. The **War Photo Gallery** is also a must, but not for the squeamish; offbeat variety is provided by the **Rupe Ethnographic Museum** and **House of Marin Držić**.

Sights & museums

Aquarium

*Damjana Jude 2, Tvrđa Sv Ivana
(020 427 937).* **Open** *Jan-Mar, Nov*
9am-1pm daily. *Apr, Oct* 9am-4pm
daily. *May* 9am-7pm daily. *June* 8am-
8pm daily. *July, Aug* 9am-9pm daily.
Sept 8am-7pm daily. **Admission** 20kn;
15kn concessions. No credit cards.
Map p49 F4 ①

Downstairs from the Maritime
Museum is this rather gloomy collection of tanks containing mainly
Mediterranean sealife: aquariums
around Europe have become so swish
these days that this sorry offering
pales in comparison. Still, it's a rare
chance to keep the kids occupied for
half an hour without having to resort
to the beach again. The sea turtle is the
most popular draw, although he looks
little happier than the motley gang of
grouper fish, sea breams and conger
eels. Bright sponges add a little colour.

Cathedral

Poljana Marina Držića (no phone).
Open 8am-8pm daily. **Admission**
treasury 7kn. No credit cards.
Map p49 D4 ②

The original church, allegedly funded
by Richard the Lionheart in recognition
of the local hospitality when shipwrecked on Lokrum in the 1190s, was
lost to the 1667 earthquake. In its place
was built a somewhat bland, baroque
affair, free but unenticing to walk
around. The main draw is the treasury
at one end, a somewhat grotesque collection of holy relics. The arm, skull
and lower leg of patron St Blaise are
kept in jewel-encrusted casings, another box contains one of Christ's nappies,
and wood from the Holy Cross is incor-
porated into a finely crafted crucifix
from the 16th century. Perhaps the
most bizarre artefact is the creepy dish
and jug designed as a gift for the
Hungarian King Mátyás Corvinus,
who died before he could receive it.

Church of Our Saviour

Stradun, by the Pile Gate (no phone).
Map p48 B2 ③

Set between the Franciscan Monastery
and the Pile Gate, facing Onofrio's
Fountain, this modest votive church
was built by Petar Andrijić in the 1520s
as a mark of gratitude following an
earthquake in 1520 itself. It has both
Gothic and Renaissance elements but
most of all, solidity, as it also survived
the more terrible earthquake of 1667.
It hosts atmospheric candlelit concerts
during the Dubrovnik Festival.

Church of St Blaise

Luža (020 411 715). **Open** *Summer*
8am-noon, 4.30-7pm daily. *Winter*
8.30am-noon, 4.30-7.30pm daily.
Admission free. **Map** p49 D3 ④

Cathedral

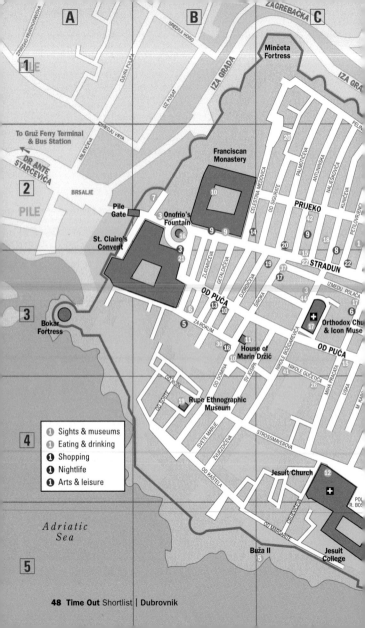

A **B** ZAGREBAČKA **C**

1

Minčeta Fortress

IZA GRA

IE IZA GRADA

To Gruž Ferry Terminal & Bus Station

DR ANTE STARČEVIĆA

BRSALJE

2 PILE

PRIJEKO

Franciscan Monastery

10

Pile Gate

Onofrio's Fountain

St. Claire's Convent

9 **9** **14**

20 **9** **18** **8**

7

16

3

21

STRADUN

ZLATARIĆEVA

GETALDIĆEVA

19 **37**

22

20 **15**

17

IZMEĐU POLAČA

3 **3** **17**

Bokar Fortress

OD PUČA

6 **13** **10**

5

ZA-ROKUM

44

17

Orthodox Chu & Icon Muse

3

ŠIROKA

DJURDJIĆEVA

30 **16**

11

House of Marin Držić

10

OD PUČA

NIKOLE BOŽIDAREVIĆA

NIKOLE GUCETIĆA

41

26

MIHA PRACATA

USKA

15

OD DOMINA

SV. JOSIPA

OD RUPA

19 Rupe Ethnographic Museum

4

SVETE MARIJE

ZVIJEZDIĆEVA

STROSSMAYEROVA

Jesuit Church **12**

OD KAŠTELA

Adriatic Sea

OD MARGARITE

ČUBRANOVIĆA

Buža II

5

5

Jesuit College

POL R. BOŠ

1 Sights & museums
1 Eating & drinking
1 Shopping
1 Nightlife
1 Arts & leisure

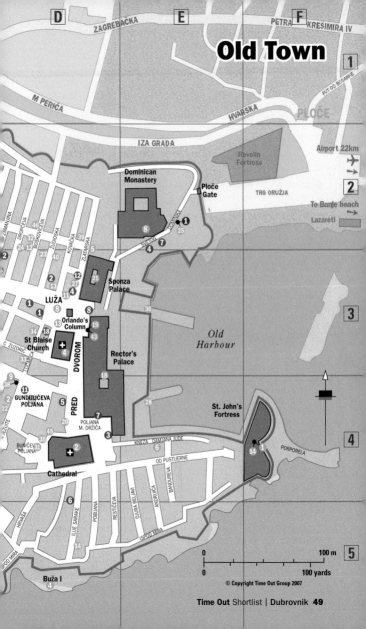

Old Town

D — ZAGREBAČKA — E — PETRA KREŠIMIRA IV — F

M PERIĆA

HVARSKA

PUT OD BOSANKE

PLOČE

IZA GRADA

Ravelin Fortress

Airport 22km ✈

TRG ORUŽJA

Dominican Monastery

Ploče Gate

To Banje beach
Lazareti

8
1 25
7
4

Sponza Palace

Old Harbour

36

Orlando's Column

19
43

Rector's Palace

St Blaise Church

18

28

St. John's Fortress

Gundulićeva Poljana

POLJANA M. DRŽIĆA

3

KNEZA DAMJANA JUDE

14
1
PORPORELA

Bunićeva Poljana

OD PUSTIJERNE

Cathedral

ILIJE SARAKE

POBIJANA

RESTIĆEVA

ĐURA BELANI

ANDRIJIĆA

BANDUREVA

ISPOD MIRA

OD PUSTIJERNE

HRVAŠA

POD MIRA

Buža I
4

0 — 100 m
0 — 100 yards

© Copyright Time Out Group 2007

Named after Dubrovnik's patron saint and set on the main square, St Blaise is ornately baroque on the outside and a sober affair within. It was built on the site of a 14th-century church 50 years after the 1667 earthquake, by Venetian architect Marino Grapelli. The must-see attraction is the altar, and its statue salvaged from the post-earthquake fire. It depicts St Blaise holding a model of the city showing how it looked in the late 1400s, with many recognisable features. The stained glass windows are a modern addition, by Ivo Dulčić.

Church of St Nicholas
Zlatarska 2 (no phone). **Open** varies. **Map** p49 D2 ⑤
Its Renaissance façade juxtaposed with the tacky, tourist restaurants along the Prijeko it bookends, this pretty little church behind the Sponza Palace was originally one of the oldest here in Dubrovnik. Renovated in 1607, it still contains original early medieval ornamentation. It's revered by locals who traditionally visit every December 6, St Nicholas Day, for a mass and a ritual blessing of apples.

Church of St Roch
Iza Roka (no phone). **Map** p48 B3 ⑥
One of the lesser known of the Old Town churches, St Roch was built in the mid 16th century in Renaissance style. Its most notable feature was not included on the architects' plans. Visible on the east wall down Getaldića is graffitied scrawl in Latin dated 1597, a warning to those playing ball here that they should realise they will all die one day. Whether it was written by one of the desperate men sentenced to death, cared for by one of the St Roch brotherhood, or by one of the brothers, we don't know. It doesn't seem to bother the children who still play ball here four centuries on.

City Walls tour
Main entrance near the Pile Gate (020 420 192). **Open** *Summer* 9am-7pm daily. *Winter* 10am-3pm daily. **Admission** 30kn; 10kn concessions. No credit cards. **Map** p48 B2 ⑦

This should be the first port of call on any visitor's agenda. The gentle stroll at your own pace atop and around Dubrovnik's battlements takes in fabulous sea views as well as stylish and sturdy 15th-century solutions to architectural conundrums. The coherent result, lapped below by the Adriatic, has withstood the earthquake of 1667, Napoleon and the Serbian shelling of 1991. See p34-37 Itineraries.

Dominican Monastery
Sv Dominika 4 (020 321 423). **Open** *Summer* 9am-6pm daily. *Winter* 9am-3pm daily. **Admission** 15kn; 7kn concessions. No credit cards. **Map** p49 E2 ⑧
Between the Sponza Palace and the Ploče Gate, this monastery is best known for its late Gothic cloisters and late 15th-century paintings of the Dubrovnik School in the museum – in particular masterpieces by Nikola Božidarević, including his *Our Lady with the Saints*. On the walls of the monastery church are a beautiful wooden crucifix by Paolo Veneziano from 1358 and a painting by renowned fin-de-siècle artist Vlaho Bukovac from Cavtat, *The Miracle of St Dominic.*

Franciscan Monastery
Stradun 2 (020 321 410/www.mala braca.hr). **Open** 9am-6pm daily. **Admission** *with Old Pharmacy* 20kn; 10kn concessions. No credit cards. **Map** p48 B2 ⑨
A real gem in the Old Town, hence the high-season hordes of noisy tourists being funnelled in, who ignore the sign of a monk making a 'shhh' gesture at the entrance. Don't be put off – try and go at the end of the day. Built in baroque design after the 1667 earthquake, whose resultant fire destroyed the works by Caravaggio, Titian and Raphael once housed in Romanesque style, this building by the Pile Gate is fronted by its one surviving external feature, a portal and pietà by the Petrović brothers. Inside, the main attraction for locals is the tablet on the north wall commemorating poet Ivan Gundulić, whose remains elsewhere in

Comedy theatre

Dubrovnik's Shakespeare provides unexpected hilarity.

A museum outlining the life and works of a Croatian-language literary giant from the 1500s – could anything be more dull?

In fact, it's quite the opposite. The bizarre **House of Marin Držić** (p54), visited almost exclusively by Croats, is a gem, and for all the wrong reasons.

Marin Držić, the Dubrovnik-born playwright of the 1500s, is a revered figure in these parts. His work is still performed today, not least as an essential part of the Dubrovnik Festival. In his day, Držić fell out with the local nobility, and exiled himself to Italy, intent on bringing down the Ragusa regime. He died penniless in Venice before he could set about it. Perhaps this museum can be considered Dubrovnik's revenge.

English-language visitors are immediately handed a retro Sony Walkman and guided round with commentary you just couldn't make up. 'By stepping onto this ground you yourself are becoming a magician,' booms a female voice, accompanied by some kind of musical interlude straight from *Blackadder*. As you walk past life-size representations of some of his most famous character creations, you are instructed to 'use your magic powers to let them speak to you' – and speak to you they do, jesters, satyrs, women representing the hand of fate. Unfortunately, it goes on for quite a while and you find yourself fast-forwarding certain sections, hoping that no one is looking.

Next up is a short film. (The DVD must be changed to your language so you may need to wait.) We discover that Držić lived in Siena which, apparently, 'is and always will be the most exciting city in Italy', struggled with debts and was nicknamed 'The Otter' due to his fondness for wearing fur. The film is presented in stern, *Open University* style by someone not unlike Ernie from *Sesame Street*.

The middle floor accommodates space-age vessels, something similar to those in *Barbarella*, and showcases photographs from the modern day. Intriguing, perhaps, but nothing to do with Držić. The top floor shows a bedroom and study, complete with table, desks and crucifixes.

It is not certain if all or any of this is authentic – but in the right mood the museum does provide classic comic moments.

Franciscan Monastery p50

here are closed off to the public. In a narrow passageway dividing the monastery from the Church of Our Saviour is the entrance to the famous Old Pharmacy (p74), still in operation after 700 years, and beautiful cloisters leading to a peaceful, petite inner garden courtyard dotted with orange trees. The numerous exhibits of the monastery's museum are located in two rooms just off the square. One contains relics relating to the Pharmacy; the other, religious artefacts such as basins for holy water, silver incense containers resembling Sunday roast gravy boats, lacework, capes and grandly embroidered cloaks, paintings, jewelled crucifixes and statues of Madonna with child. A number of reliquaries hold the remains of saints, some shaped as a not-so saintly single upright finger. Unfortunately, you can't see where the monks ate and slept but it's well worth a look.

Franciscan Monastery Old Pharmacy Museum

Stradun 2 (020 321 410/www.mala braca.hr). **Open** 9am-6pm daily. **Admission** *with Monastery* 20kn; 10kn concessions. No credit cards. **Map** p48 B2 ⑩

One of the oldest in Europe – if not *the* oldest – this pharmacy near the main door of the Franciscan Monastery is a working chemists. Old locals totter in for their regular prescriptions as tourists peruse the jars and vessels from yesteryear. Most local sources give the date of the pharmacy's foundation as 1317 – all records were burned in the fire after the 1667 earthquake. Many of the containers and poisons you see date from the 15th century. Also on display, in one of the museum rooms leading off from the courtyard through the back, are disturbingly large grinders and other implements, giving a perspective to our moaning about modern health systems. While medicine has improved, the prescription book shows us that doctors' handwriting has obviously gone the other way.

High and dry

The **Rupe Ethnographic Museum** (p57) is a little-known attraction two minutes up from Stradun, a handy diversion from the sights and crowds below.

This former granary, opened in 1590 after 42 years of work, sits up a hill – high means dry. Turn around before you enter, and enjoy the view: your back is to the sea and you're facing the mountains. From here you can study the stream of ant-sized tourists circling the City Walls.

The Rupe was where grain was stored in 15 large wells (*rupe* means 'holes') hewn from rock, coated with impermeable mortar. It held 1,200 tonnes of grain, the centre of the local food administration system, ensuring the rapidly rising population could all be fed. Grain was dried and aired in the upper floors then channelled down huge chutes to the stores below, then sold to the public.

This space now houses the Ethnographic Museum, showing how locals used to live. This remit makes it more down to earth than rector's robes and angelic madonnas. There are mosaics of boats, lions and doves. A floor dedicated to traditional farming tools and techniques shows olive-oil grindstones, wicker baskets, rusty guns and old hoes. There are festive peasant costumes, painted eggs and a selection of weird lute-like instruments. It's all quite fun before you step outside again to take in that breathtaking view – and all the crowds that come with it.

House of Marin Držić

Široka ulica 7 (020 323 242). **Open**
Summer 9am-6pm daily. *Winter* 9am-
2pm Mon-Sat. **Admission** 35kn; 15kn
concessions. No credit cards.
Map p48 B3 ⓫

Apart from his plays, religiously performed every summer at the
Dubrovnik Festival, only patchy
details remain of the life of Croatia's
most celebrated playwright, who died
shortly after Shakespeare was born.
This most unusual theatrical museum,
set up in the 1990s, fills in the gaps by
illustrating this local writer's life and
works with a series of models and
mock-ups. See box p51.

Jesuit Church &
Jesuit College

*Uz Jezuite/poljana Rudjera Boškovića
(no phone).* **Open** varies. Admission
free. **Map** p49 C5 ⓬

Dominating the Old Town from atop
its grand staircase, the Jesuit Church
was built in baroque style by fellow
Jesuit Andrea Pozzo, also responsible
for his signature trompe l'oeil features
at the original Il Gesù in Rome, and the
Jesuit Church in Vienna, where he is
buried. Construction on it began in
fateful 1667, the year of the earthquake,
and therefore it wasn't completed until
many decades later, in 1725. Corinthian
columns stand sternly facing the pleasingly haphazard square of poljana
Rudjera Boškovića. Behind them, an
interior displays scenes from the life of
St Ignatius, the Basque soldier who
founded the Jesuits in the 1530s. You'll
find the church also referred to as St
Ignatius. It forms part of the Collegium
Ragusinum complex, including the
Jesuit College, where generations of
prominent Dubrovnik men of arts and
letters were educated. The staircase,
which bookends two sides of tourist
restaurants leading to the open market
square of Gundulićeva poljana, was
completed by Pietro Passalacqua in the
1730s. It stands comparison with the
Spanish Steps in Rome, built around
the same time – Passalacqua happened
to be Roman.

Luža

Map p49 D3 ⓭

If Dubrovnik has a main square, it's
this, an open space heading the main
street of Stradun. Surrounded by terrace cafés and the key sights of the
Sponza Palace and the Church of St
Blaise, adjoining at right-angles Pred
Dvorom and the Rector's Palace, Luža
has attractions of its own. Its centrepiece is Orlando's Column, a statue of
Charlemagne's warrior and literary
hero Roland. It's as landmark as you
can get – all state declarations were
read out from its base and Roland's
forearm was a unit of measurement in
the construction of all the buildings
you see around you. A faint line still
runs beneath Roland's feet. Behind the
column stands the Clock Tower, built
in 1446 and restored over the centuries.
The time is told by a modern digital
clock in blue numerals and, on the
hour, the twin bronze figures of Maro
and Baro. Their 15th-century originals
are in the Sponza Palace.

Maritime Museum

Damjana Jude 2 (020 323 904). **Open**
May-Oct 9am-6pm daily. *Nov-Mar* 9am-
2pm Tue-Sun. **Admission** 35kn. No
credit cards. **Map** p49 F4 ⓮

The Maritime Museum shares the
same building, St John's Fortress, as
the Aquarium, its courtyard entrance
lined with small cannons and huge
anchors. Two floors of artefacts are
divided between the very old (books,
paintings of ships and their captains,
swords, atlases and early scientific
equipment such as quadrants) and the
old, 19th- and 20th-century pieces. One
wall has images of the 1991 bombing.
Although ship-focused, the museum
handily guides you through the development of Dubrovnik as a town via its
trading routes and partners.

Mosque

Miha Pracata. **Open** 10am-1pm daily.
Map p48 C3 ⓯

On the corner of Miha Pracata and Od
Puča, close to the Serbian Orthodox
Church, Dubrovnik's modest mosque

serves the handful of local muslims – there isn't much to see for visitors. Plans to build a much bigger mosque overlooking the Old Town were rejected by the city council.

Onofrio's Fountain

Poljana Paška Miličevića.
Map p48 B2 ⑯

At the Pile Gate end of Stradun, the Great Fountain erected by Neapolitan engineer Onofrio della Cava in 1444 was part of an elaborate local water supply light years ahead of most of what was passing for sanitation in Europe at the time. The water was sourced from some 12 miles away at Rijeka Dubrovačka. Although much of the ornate upper part was lost to the 1667 earthquake, the Great Fountain retains its polygonal shape and 16 carved heads from which water still pours. It's a popular landmark and meeting place. Its aesthetically pleasing appearance was due to the work of Milanese architect Pietro di Martino.

Della Cava and di Martino also created the Smaller Fountain at the other end of Stradun, beneath the clock tower.

Orthodox Church & Icon Museum

Od Puča 8 (020 323 823). **Open**
Church 9am-4pm daily. *Museum* 9am-2pm Mon-Sat. **Admission** *Museum* 10kn. No credit cards. **Map** p48 C3 ⑰

Right in the heart of the Old Town, built in the late 19th century, this Serbian church is one of the plainer ones, inside and out, of those in the region. The fact that it is here at all, intact, after the horrors of 1991, speaks volumes about Dubrovnik. You can find a more colourful collection of icons a couple of doors down at a modest two-room museum accessed up a flight of stairs through the entrance to the jewellery shop Djardin. One room contains a hotchpotch of icons, Balkan and Russian, from varying centuries; in another, there's a series of portraits of eminent local Serbs by Vlaho Bukovac.

DUBROVNIK BY AREA

War through the lens

Dubrovnik's best gallery has a global focus.

Portraits of Iraq, Afghanistan, the recent Lebanon conflict – these are the themes for 2007 at Dubrovnik's striking contemporary gallery, **War Photo Limited** (p80). It's a vital venue, not just in local terms but, because of what it displays, internationally. The fact that many of its exhibitions tour is most appropriate.

Devotedly managed since its opening in 2003 by New Zealand war photographer Wade Goddard, who came here in the early 1990s and stayed, the gallery could have easily limited its focus to the conflict going on here in the city. But Goddard quickly expanded its remit to exhibit work by some of the world's leading exponents of this brave art, illustrating flash points around the world.

Much thought, guided by a photographer's eye, is given to space and light. WPL has a contemplative atmosphere; you feel miles away from the Stradun crowds. The two-floor venue is practical, too, doubling up as a conference centre in the off months of January and February.

The first floor houses the current exhibition. The second is home to highlights from previous shows and, of course, the 1990s war in Yugoslavia. Viewing images of shells and fires raging in the Old Town, a place that today seems completely serene but for the constant patter of tourists' footsteps, is disconcerting. You can even sit and watch slow-paced slide shows on large TV screens.

Beware – it's not easy viewing. The 2006 exhibition on Liberia was the hardest hitting yet: a photograph of a decapitated head produced audible gasps. Do not let this put you off – these images are real, the wars and the victims are real, and this is what we now term 'collateral damage'. It is steeling, challenging but ultimately positive, and you leave feeling very lucky and energised to help.

Photojournalists have risked their lives to deliver these images. Work is sold as limited edition prints for 10,000kn (1,350 euros). You can also note comments in the visitors' book. 'It moved me beyond words' is typical.

Rector's Palace

Pred Dvorom 3 (020 321 497). **Open**
Summer 9am-6pm daily. *Winter* 9am-
2pm daily. **Admission** 20kn; 7kn. No
credit cards. **Map** p49 D3 ⑱

The most historic monument in all
Dubrovnik, the Rector's Palace was
rebuilt twice. The first, by Onofrio della
Cava of fountain fame, was in
Venetian-Gothic style, visible in the
window design once you ascend the
grand staircase to the Rector's living
quarters. The second time was by
Florentine Michelozzo Michelozzi,
responsible for much of the City Wall
and here, the loggia façade. On the
ground floor, either side of a light-filled
courtyard, are the prison and court-
rooms of the Ragusa Republic, and a
separate exhibition of Neolithic Age
findings from the Vela Špilja on
Korčula. More Neolithic and Bronze
Age finds from Gudnja Cave near Ston
are on display upstairs. Here, where
each Rector resided for his month's
stint, is a strange assortment of items:

sedan chairs, carriages, magistrates'
robes and wigs, portraits of local notables and Ivo Rudenjak's beautifully
carved bookcase, in the otherwise staid
reception and administration rooms.
One curiosity is the clocks, some set at
quarter to six, the exact time when
Napoleon's troops entered in 1806.

Rupe Ethnographic Museum

Od Rupa (020 412 545). **Open**
Summer 9am-6pm daily. *Winter* 9am-
2pm Mon-Fri. **Admission** 35kn; 15kn
concessions. No credit cards. **Map**
p48 B4 ⑲

Rupe, or 'holes', refer to those dotting
this spacious granary that once fed
Dubrovnik. Today it houses a modest
ethnographic museum on the top floor,
containing peasant costumes and items
depicting life in the countryside. Most
of all, it offers a fabulous view of the
Old Town, complemented by the sea on
one side and mountains on the other.
See box p53.

Orthodox Church p55

Sigurata Convent Museum

Od Sigurate 13 (020 321 467). **Open**
July, Aug 10am-noon, 4-6pm daily. *Jan-
June, Sep-Dec* by appointment only.
Admission 10kn; 5kn concessions.
No credit cards. **Map** p48 C2 ⑳

For the visitor used to modern-day
attractions, the peculiar timelessness of
the petite, pink-façaded Sigurata
Convent will make a considerable
impression. Such places are harder and
harder to find. The hospitality of the
Franciscan sisters of the Third Order
is traditional and it's not unusual for
one of them to present personally the
rarities of their collection. Spread over
three rooms in the basement and the
first floor, attractions include a gilded
processional crucifix from the 14th century, and a variety of household uten-
sils, cake moulds, sewing kits, and so
on, used by nuns down the centuries.

Sponza Palace

Luža (020 321 032). **Open** 9.15am-
2.15pm daily. **Admission** free.
Map 49 D3 ㉑

The attractive, 16th-century former
customs house and Ragusa mint is
used to house the extensive state
archives (by appointment only, phone

ahead) and temporary exhibitions. Free
to enter, a current long-term exhibition
has been given space in a small room
opposite the ticket office: the Memorial
Room of the Dubrovnik Defenders.
Covering the terrible 12 months from
October 1991 (although keen to point
out that isolated attacks continued
until the summer of 1995), the exhibition contains portraits of the 300
defenders and civilians who died during the siege and the tattered remnant
of the Croatian flag that flew atop
strategic Mount Srdj.

Stradun

Map pp48-49 B2-D2 ㉒

The heart and spine of Dubrovnik, only
292 metres long, runs between the
gates of Pile and Ploče, bookended by
Onofrio's fountains. Placa, as it is also
called (addresses of the many shops
and businesses along it still use this
more traditional name), is eminently
strollable. The smooth white stones,
repaved in 1901, glint in the morning
sun and slide under the feet after a rain-
storm. The street was originally a
channel that separated the mainland
from an islet, and the Slav community

Rector's Palace p57

from the Italianate one. Silted up and filled in from the 11th century, Stradun thus united the two halves of Dubrovnik. Once of red brick and lined with Renaissance palaces, Stradun was renovated after the earthquake of 1667 by Giulio Cerrutio , who created its regular appearance that you see today. Uniform buildings, nearly all with a shop at street level and green-shuttered windows above, line the street, interspersed with café terraces. Each of the two dozen street corners are graced with a maroon flag in faux-historic style, listing the shops, bars and restaurants you'll find up the next turning. They are regularly updated too. This is useful for streets north of Stradun, as the climb up the stairs can be steep. Barkers from tourist-trap Prijeko restaurants work this northern flank. There are always tour group leaders gabbling away in foreign languages to their attentive flocks and always, but always, somebody filming.

Synagogue

Žudioska 5 (020 321 028). **Open** 10am-8pm Mon-Fri. **Admission** 10kn. No credit cards. **Map** p49 D2 ㉓

Situated in the old Jewish ghetto, Europe's second oldest synagogue is worth visiting for its fascinating two-room museum. There are ceremonial horns, prayer books and Torah pointers but the real treasure is the documentation. You can trace the arrival from Spain of the first registered Jewish citizen (in 1421), through full Jewish emancipation in 1808, to the seemingly innocent Croatian government official paper of the 1940s. Here in the shocking simplicity of black and white, we see the confiscation of Jewish property, the forced identification of Jewish stores, the restriction of movement and gatherings, and the compulsory wearing of badges and armbands. Croatia was a willing fascist ally, it had concentration camps and Jews were taken to them. This is a stark reminder of something that is little discussed these days.

Eating & drinking

Africa

Vetranićeva 3 (098 854 954 mobile). **Open** 5pm-1am daily. **Bar**. No credit cards. **Map** p48 C3 ➊

One of the busier spots come midnight in the Old Town, Africa attracts a young crowd who squeeze into a compact, colourful space of well conceived murals, wood carvings of thin faces and bar tables topped with maps of the continent concerned. Nothing much African on the menu, though – just 50 odd cocktails, shooters, short and long drinks, plus Karlovačko and Heineken on draught. Watch out for darts flying into the machine board by the bar. Under the same umbrella as the nearby nightlife hub, the Casablanca.

Arka

Gundulićeva poljana (no phone). **Open** 11am-midnight daily. **Restaurant.** **Map** p49 D4 ❷

Not the most adventurous restaurant in Dubrovnik, that's true, but Arka is well situated at the foot of the grand staircase below the Sv Ignacio church on this busy market square. It's also able to serve up mounds of shellfish reasonably quickly should the occasion arise. Platters for two are the way to go, it seems. Pastas are a speciality too, in particular lasagne, and there are (for Croatia) plenty of choices for vegetarians. Considering the location, they could easily charge more.

Baracuda

Nikole Božidarevića 10 (020 323 160). **Open** 10.30am-12.30am daily. **Restaurant.** **Map** p48 C3 ❸

This small, friendly pizzeria near the Serbian Orthodox church was one of the first to open in Dubrovnik. The portions here are enormous, the prices are reasonable and unless you're particularly discerning about your crusts or organic toppings, everyone comes away happy. Baracuda II in Lapad, on Ispod Petke, benefits from a roof terrace and proximity to the beach.

Buža I

Accessed from Ilije Sarake (no phone). **Open** *Summer* 8am-late daily. No credit cards. **Bar.** **Map** p49 D5 ❹

Dubrovački kantun p63

The more haphazard of the two 'Buža' open-air bars cut into the rocks supporting the City Walls, Buža I was closed in the winter of 2006, promised to open in the spring. Sunbathing and diving into the sea are still possible from the planed flat surfaces – clamber out using the steps cut into the rocks. See box p62.

Buža II

Crijevićeva 9 (no phone). **Open** 10am-late daily. **Bar**. No credit cards. **Map** p48 C5 ⑤

The more well known of the cliff-face bars, this one is well organised, with signs ('Cold Drinks') placed by the Jesuit Church and along Od Margarite. A straw roof protects customers from the open sun by day; fabulous sunsets ensure that all the tables are full in high season. See box p62.

Carpe Diem

Kneza Damjana Jude 4 (no phone). **Open** 5pm-1am daily. **Bar**. No credit cards. **Map** p49 E4 ⑥

Down the same street as the Aquarium, this neat, stylish, narrow bar attracts a young party crowd away from Stradun with a lively offering of dance and domestic pop tunes, cheap but by no means nasty cocktails and a pleasing lack of foreign tourists. Sometimes opens for breakfast coffees in summer.

Casablanca

Zamanjina 7 (no phone). **Open** 5.30pm-1am daily. **Bar**. No credit cards. **Map** p49 D3 ⑦

Reasonable candidate for best bar in the Old Town – certainly it's the most spacious and tastefully decorated, providing the most interesting DJ sounds of the lot. Old film and beer ads brighten the main space, bookended by a long bar counter above which beckon publicity posters from Olympic Games long gone and pool-table lightshades of coloured glass advertising Coors beer. Cocktails come in creamy or killer varieties, football and beer videos play on the large TV screen and the staff buzz about in daft blue shirts with some bullshit motto on them. Recommended.

Fickle fame

At the height of her fame, Liz Taylor is in town with Richard Burton, a VIP couple feted by Tito. Attention is low-key. At one point Liz wants to walk down Stradun but fears hassle. She plucks up courage, walks up and down – and nothing happens. As she starts to worry she has lost her cachet, Liz is approached by an *originalo*, a local bohemian intellectual, with a piece of paper and pen. Liz asks him what she should do. 'Nothing,' he says, signing the paper and passing it to her. 'I just wanted to give you my autograph.'

Fame is a fickle game. Today local newsstands are crammed with celebrity mags. A visitor half the stature of Liz is paparazzi'ed into an early night. For older locals, it's embarrassing.

In Dubrovnik Airport's official *Passenger Guide*, photos of random arrivals – Don King, a Saudi prince, unnamed Chinese VIPs – express an odd sense of self-worth. Locals are delighted by the constant appearance of Croatophile John Malkovich but shocked at the millions he paid for a villa here. Daily rumours surround how much foreign stars pay for property. Demand is outstripping supply. Is Dubrovnik building a golf course? A marina for large yachts? A heliport?

As the Old Town empties of locals and property prices past Monaco levels, Dubrovnik still craves celebrity recognition – but hasn't thought through the consequences of the international jet-set invasion.

The hole in the wall gang

Cliff-face bars provide respite from crowded cafés.

Buža II

Far from the downtown flock, five minutes along a back alley, the bar table of your dreams is set on one of two panoramic terraces atop a rocky sea-view promontory propping up the city walls: **Buža I** (p60) and **Buža II** (p61). Find your niche, gawp at the awesome sunset and sip a three-euro beer. At No.I, you can even dive naked into a moonlit Adriatic.

Buža, meaning 'hole in the wall', suits boozers, swimmers and sunbathers alike. Of the two, Buža I is the most basic but perhaps the most enjoyable – maybe because of easy access to and from the sea, via metal steps fixed to the rocks. From the cathedral, walk down Ilije Sarake as far as the dining terrace of the Konoba Ekvinocijo. Diagonally opposite is a doorway saying simply '8-20'. Duck in to find the words 'Topless Nudist' on the wall. Negotiate the stone staircase and behold! At differing levels according to the rock formation, tables appear –

as does a bar counter and, sadly, Sadé. Somehow they're always playing Sadé. Yet not even Sadé can ruin this moonlit moment.

Buža II is the better known. It has a straw roof, waiters in logoed T-shirts and dinky wooden trays. From the open square of Rudjera Boškovića, by the Jesuit church, follow a sign saying 'Cold Drinks With The Most Beautiful View'. Walk along the passage, across a makeshift football pitch. Ahead an arrow points to 'Cold Drinks'. The cold drinks here are Ožujsko and Heineken, although many prefer wine, Malvazija or Babić, all about 30kn. Buža II attracts an older crowd, who put their feet up on the railing separating shoe sole from sheer drop. Elvis or Gene Pitney is the music *du choix*.

The authorities are said to scorn these rough diamonds. Buža I briefly closed in 2006 but will reopen in 2007. Join the Hole in the Wall gang before the whole shooting match goes up.

Cele Café

Stradun 1 (no phone). **Open** 9am-midnight daily. **Café**. No credit cards. **Map** p49 D3 ⑧

Tucked in by St Blaise Church, this busy little place forms a ring of cafés around the main square of Luža. Somewhat overshadowed by the graĐskavana and Dubrava opposite, the Cele will undergo a pre-season renovation in the early spring of 2007 under new owner Robert Zanetić, who runs a number of venues in the city. If the new management has any sense it should up the salary of the pastry chef, creator of the wonderful gooey, sugary cakes on offer throughout the day.

Defne

Pucić Palace Hotel, Od Puča 1 (020 326 200/www.thepucicpalace.com). **Open** *May-Oct* 11am-midnight daily. **Restaurant**. **Map** p49 D4 ⑨

Defne occupies the roof terrace of the Old Town's five-star hotel, one of three restaurants. Chef Ozgur Donertas creates flavoursome meat options from Turkey and the Levant as well as maritime ones from closer to home. Mljet lobster is grilled with a white wine risotto or poached with black risotto and saffron sauce. Defne prides itself on its traditional seafood soup with real sea stone – the edible contents are fresh seafood and garden vegetables. Toddle downstairs after a memorable meal only 300kn lighter.

Domino

Od Domina 6 (020 323 103). **Open** *Apr-Oct* 11am-midnight daily. **Restaurant**. **Map** p48 B3 ⑩

Always packed in summer, this steakhouse occupies an entire courtyard on the south side of Stradun. There's not just meat – though you won't find better at this price in town – but seafood and shellfish too. The air-conditioned stone interior provides welcome relief from the tourist groups outside.

Dubrava

Stradun (no phone). **Open** 8.45am-midnight daily. **Café**. No credit cards. **Map** p49 D3 ⑪

One of a handful of decent choices for that first coffee near the main square, Dubrava catches the morning sun and offers the most choice from its thick, bound drinks menu. Coffees, chocolates and children's cappuccinos are complemented by draught Laško light and dark, Guinness, 15 cocktails at 35kn-40kn, house wine at 80kn a litre, plus Pošip, Dingač and other quality labels. There's food too: breakfasts, omelettes, seasonal or seafood salads, even spaghettis and steaks.

Dubrovački kantun

Boškovićeva 5 (020 331 911/091 699 4966 mobile). **Open** 10.30am-4pm, 6.30pm-midnight daily. **Restaurant**. **Map** p49 D3 ⑫

Andrej Di Leo's delightful little eaterie makes superb use of healthy local vegetables, meats and cheeses – rocket is used in abundance almost year-round. A cosy interior decorated with strings of garlic and quaint old finds accommodates 27 covers – book in summer. Dive straight into a Dubrovački kantun platter (99kn for two) of smoked ham, cheeses, anchovies and rocket or opt for Dalmatian-style cod (55kn) as a starter or main (90kn), with seasonal vegetables. In winter, the house beef stew *paštticada* (80kn) comes into its own. Dalmatian flans (15kn) follow. Superior sandwiches are sold in summer. Great staff, highly recommended.

Dundo Maroje

Kovačka/Stradun (020 321 445). **Open** 11am-midnight daily. **Restaurant**. **Map** p49 D3 ⑬

Open all year round, this intimate, traditional konoba near the main square does nothing revolutionary but what it does do – lamb shashliks, grilled squids, more fish choice than most – it does well. Certainly, the kitchen seems to know how much garlic and oil to add where necessary. There are a couple of children's choices on the menu, plus enticing desserts such as pear in red wine, and hot bananas. Starters include Croatian cheeses and lesser found offerings like lobster carpaccio.

DUBROVNIK BY AREA

Ekvinocijo

Ilije Sarake 10 (020 420 626).
Open *Summer* 10am-midnight
daily. **Restaurant**. **Map** p49 D5 ⑭
Set away from the tourist bustle in the
heart of the Old Town, this traditional
terrace *konoba* turns out standard
domestic fare with a smile. It's handy
for those using the sunbathing terrace
cut into the cliff-face of the city walls –
the doorway is diagonally opposite this
modest courtyard. Squid, scampi,
seafood risottos, it's all the kind of ideal
Mediterranean fare you need for a post-
swim lunch. Closed in winter.

Festival Café

Stradun 28 (020 321 148). **Open**
10am-midnight daily. **Café**.
Map p48 C3 ⑮
Landmark venue towards the Pile end
of Stradun. Pricy even by Dubrovnik
standards, but if you're willing to pay
55kn for an Ice Festival (Cointreau,
Blue Curaçao, lime) or 42kn for a
Festival sandwich of smoked ham, brie
and tomato, then settle in for proper
service and comfort. It's got a proper
bar counter too, a long interior brightened by old Cinzano ads and outdoor
seating on Stradun. Fruit frappés and
home-made cakes complete the picture.

fresh*

Vetranićeva 4 (091 896 7509 mobile/
www.igotfresh.com). **Open** *Summer*
9am-1am daily. *Winter* 6pm-midnight
Tue-Thur; 6pm-1am Fri, Sat. **Café**.
Map p48 C3 ⑯
Friendly and bright, this small bar-café
run 'for travellers by travellers' has
branched out from its Korčula base
into Dubrovnik. An odd, pricy choice
of location, perhaps – backpackers
don't swarm here. Then again, there's
little competition for the daily detoxes
of juices, smoothies and wraps, and
evening retoxes of beers and cocktails.

Gaffe Pub

Miha Pracata 4 (020 323 867). **Open**
10am-11pm daily. **Bar**. **Map** p48 C3 ⑰
The unfortunately named Gaffe comprises a corridor terrace and shiny
wood interior with little booths. Hajduk

Split and Everton football souvenirs
lend a suitably sporting touch, while DJ
decks provide conversation-level entertainment. Strongbow and Guinness are
among the draught options. Kodak
snaps nod towards the concept of a regular clientele, aided by the growing
number of expat residents propping up
the bar. Local prices levied on local
brews, Karlovačko at 12kn a glass, for
example. Happy hour 5-7pm.

Galerie

Kunićeva 7 (no phone). **Open** noon-
midnight daily. **Bar**. No credit cards.
Map p48 C2 ⑱
A rather stylish off-Stradun option,
popular with a young party crowd, and
ideal for a pre-club couple of swifties.
Chat-friendly rap and dance music fills
a modest interior decorated with striking line drawings by Nikolina
Šimunović, while friends relax in the
wicker chairs at the back. Brown stools
surround a busy bar counter that dis-
penses standard cocktails and draught
Laško. A better option than the dozens
of tourist-filled spots nearby.

graDskavana

Luža 2 (020 321 414/www.mea-culpa.
hr). **Open** *Summer* 8am-2am daily.
Winter 8am-11pm daily. **Café**.
Map p49 D3 ⑲
This was once a landmark coffeehouse
echoing a bygone era, a meeting place
where locals spent hours observing
each other. A modern revamp has
brought in neat red-and-blue chairs on
the prominent terrace; the interior of
wrought-iron and pastel colours has
lost the decorative fuss of yesteryear.
Drinks, too, have caught up with contemporary mores – there's a handful of
cocktails at 70kn. You'll find a similar
selection in the adjoining Taverna
Arsenal, under the same umbrella.

Hemingway Bar

Pred Dvorom (no phone). **Open** noon-
1am daily. **Bar**. **Map** p49 D4 ⑳
Prominent cocktail bar opposite the
Rector's Palace offering the most com-
prehensive range of drinks in the Old
Town. Pleasingly and surprisingly,

nearly all are in the 50kn bracket, with the option of 150kn-200kn pitchers for four. No real surprises among the selection, Daiquiris and Mojitos mixed with Havana 3, plus the house combination of Pernod and champagne in a Death in the Afternoon. Expect a pleasant buzz around the bar and terrace.

Jadran

Poljana Paška Miličevića 1 (020 429 325). **Open** 10am-midnight daily. **Restaurant. Map** p48 B3 ㉑

Near the Pile Gate, this rather sturdy, mid-priced restaurant makes the best of its location in the old Convent of St Claire, placing diners in a pretty courtyard. The menu is standard – grilled meats, squid, salads, fish of the day – but the setting overshadows the sense of familiarity. A lovely interior too, should all the tables outside be taken.

Kamenice

Gundlićeva poljana 8 (020 323 685/ 020 421 499). **Open** *Apr-Oct* 7am-10pm daily. *Nov-Mar* 7am-4pm daily. **Restaurant.** No credit cards. **Map** p49 D4 ㉒

Timeless, traditional and tremendous – and cheap – the locals' favourite has hardly changed despite the tourist traps around it. A prime site by the market has certainly not affected pricing policy, decor or staff dress. 1970s' era waitresses in mules deliver piles of mussels (46kn), squid (57kn) and little fish (46kn) in white-tile surroundings. Oysters too, hence the name. Watch out for early winter closing times.

Karaka Irish bar

Izmedju Polača 5 (020 323 070/www. irishpub-karaka.t-com.hr). **Open** noon-1am daily. **Bar. Map** p48 C3 ㉓

This long-established expat bar stands beside another, the Gaffe Pub. Locally-owned Karaka comprises a compact interior filled with pub paraphernalia and two large television screens, the focus of attention on sports nights. There are a couple of tables outside too. Erdinger, Kilkenny and Guinness are among the foreign and domestic beers. Many remain after the mid-afternoon happy hours to close of play – you'll be lucky to find a spot after 10pm.

Kamenice

In a class of its own

2006 hit Wanda shines amid the tourist-trap eateries.

'You can flip every menu upside down and they will all still be the same,' said restaurateur Goran Starčić, describing the tourist-trap eateries that plague Dubrovnik's main dining drag of Prijeko. 'With Wanda we were looking to create something different.'

A native of Dubrovnik, Goran opened **Wanda** (p72) in 2006 after 15 years in the restaurant industry in Los Angeles. Overnight success has encouraged the opening of sister venue **Surf & Turf** (p71) in the spring of 2007.

In both the Western influence shows – although neither is brash. At Wanda, Goran and his team, including his Swedish wife he met here in 1979, put together simple, well-conceived Mediterranean cuisine using fresh, locally found ingredients. Goran leaves early every morning to the fish and produce markets. 'Storage can be a real problem here,' explains Goran. 'Space is pretty limited. We have to buy in every day.'

Diners shouldn't worry. An enticing Italianate menu, divided into soups, appetisers, salads, risottos, first and second courses, impresses with its deft touches: the extra virgin olive oil in the warm seafood salad; the raspberry vinaigrette dressing the salad of salmon and artichoke; the light vodka sauce combining with the salmon in the farfalle pasta, the hint of cream sherry and red wine to bring out the spinach and ricotta taste of the tortellini. Rocket is used throughout, most effectively with the mixed lentils and tomato beneath the John Dory, and mingled with Parmesan in the beef carpaccio.

Service is as important as the food being presented. 'From our experience in America I know that you need good staff to create the right atmosphere, as well as the freshest ingredients, the best wine, and so on. It's all about repeat business, word of mouth, recommendations to friends.'

Repeat business is alien to Prijeko. Diners, drummed up by barkers working Stradun below, are crammed onto terrace tables and given picture menus to point at. They won't be poisoned or cheated, but they're not expected to return. Maximum profit is wrung from wine, cheese and extras.

Goran located here by chance – the premises were vacant – but it's no coincidence that Wanda is drawing discerning diners down the street, away from the dross.

Katie O'Connor's Irish Pub

Dropčeva 4A (020 321 575). **Open** 9am-2am Mon-Thur, Sun; 9am-3am Fri, Sat. **Bar**. **Map** p49 D3 ㉔

The best of the Irish venues is also the most recently opened, an Australian-Croatian operation – look out for the board announcing that week's Sky Sports matches on the right-hand side halfway up Dropčeva. Within, downstairs, is a cavern-like space decked out in wooden benches, green cushions and framed old Guinness ads. On offer are all-day breakfasts, fish and chips in Guinness batter and sundry pub meals until 6pm, complemented by draught Harp, Erdinger, Kilkenny, Laško, Strongbow and the black stuff.

Labirint

Sv Dominika (020 322 222/www. labirint-dubrovnik.com). **Open** noon-midnight daily. **Restaurant**. **Map** p49 E2 ㉕

After years of renovation and refurbishment, this prime space opened again in 2005. Bar, restaurant and nightclub (p78), the Labirint boasts a fabulous setting, overlooking the old harbour from the Sv Luka battlement. The restaurant does a decent job at sometimes twice the price levied elsewhere. Standard pastas, grilled meats and fish dishes are served in the stone alcoves or on the starry terrace, but it's the setting you're paying for – and the setting (and the bill) you'll be talking about afterwards.

Lanterna

Nikole Gučetića (no phone). **Open** 9am-11pm daily. **Restaurant**. No credit cards. **Map** p48 C3 ㉖

Tucked away down a tiny alleyway, this modest, reasonably-priced eaterie makes a welcome change from the more brash and pricy establishments nearby. Dalmatian *pašticada*, a local marinated beef stew, is well worth the 65kn on colder days. Breaded goat's cheese is another recommendation and there is a long list of pasta and rice dishes at under 50kn. You'll find a decent array of local wines too.

Libertina

Zlatarska 3 (no phone). **Open** noon-midnight daily. **Bar**. No credit cards. **Map** p49 D3 ㉗

This characterful shoebox of a bar is known as 'Luci' after Luci Capurso, owner and ex-member of legendary locals Dubrovački Trubaduri. His old bandmate runs the busy Troubador, but this is off the tourist track. There's just enough room for an Ožujsko beer-tap, a Gaggia coffee machine, retro souvenirs and cuttings from the glory years. Luci serves the regulars, pleasingly oblivious to the money being made at inferior bars nearby.

Lokanda Peskarija

Na Ponti (020 324 750). **Open** 8am-midnight daily. **Restaurant**. No credit cards. **Map** p49 E4 ㉘

Queues form around the old harbour for good domestic dishes at knock-down prices swiftly served by over-worked staff. Tables overlook bobbing boats or stand in a two-floor rustic interior. A modest menu includes seafood risottos and grilled squid at 50kn-70kn, plus equally cheap but drinkable draught domestic wine (7kn/70kn). Unusually, there are also quality wines by the glass (Dingač 32kn). A local motto over the door says: 'Here we eat, drink and party.' Exactly.

Ludwig

Zamanjina 7 (no phone). **Open** noon-midnight daily. **Bar**. No credit cards. **Map** p48 C3 ㉙

Even this grunge bar in a Stradun side street has its own dinky little lantern, although you can't see any middle-aged couples writing postcards. Gogol, Mogwai, *Kill Bill* and Hendrix all get a decorative nod, but it's the hard-living drinkers hunched around the counter that make the place. Unthreatening if entertainingly edgy, Ludwig offers welcome respite from the dainty tourist traps nearby.

Mea Culpa

Za Rokom 3 (020 323 430/www.mea-culpa.hr). **Open** 9am-midnight daily. **Restaurant**. **Map** p48 B3 ㉚

DUBROVNIK BY AREA

Run by the same management as the Lokanda Peskarija (p67), this is generally considered the best pizzeria in town. It certainly serves the biggest pizzas. It's a simple wooden venue at the Pile Gate end of the Old Town, providing a straightforward 50kn dining fix. If you don't fancy pizza, there's also grilled meats to choose from. With tables outside on a summer's eve, Mea Culpa makes for a pleasant, cheap and communal dining choice.

Mirage

Buničeva poljana 3 (020 323 489). **Open** 9am-1am daily. **Bar**. No credit cards. **Map** p49 D4 ③①
One of a group of cafés making this dual-courtyard area the centrepiece of Old Town nightlife in summer, Mirage and its expansive terrace deal with the overflow from the invariably choca Troubador (p71) across the square. Its beers, wines and cocktails are cheaper, too, and there's a friendly buzz around the comfortable bar interior in the shoulder seasons.

Netcafé

Prijeko 21 (020 321 025/www.net cafe.hr). **Open** *Summer* 9am-1am daily. *Winter* 9am-11pm daily. **Café**. **Map** p49 D2 ③②
Not the cheapest spot in town (7.5kn) or the most spacious – hardly any room for elbows or papers – but the Netcafé is certainly the most convenient place to check your mail, towards the end of the street lined with tourist restaurants. It's air-conditioned, has plenty of computers and serves decent coffee. You can also scan, copy, print, fax and, if you need, connect your own laptop.

Oliva

Lučarica 5 (020 324 594). **Open** 11am-midnight daily. **Restaurant**. **Map** p49 D3 ③③
As good as any in town, this neat, orange-tinted pizzeria near the main square offers the best choices for vegetarians from the two dozen pizzas on the menu. Tables outside in summer, able, reasonably lively staff, simple understated decor of wooden furniture,

a tiled floor and framed pictures on the wall – yet Oliva is invariably overlooked by punters for the Baracuda or more tourist-oriented establishments. A mystery, really.

Penatur

Lučarica 2 (020 323 700). **Open** 11.30am-11pm daily. **Restaurant**. **Map** p49 D3 ③④
This modest place isn't a bad or expensive choice for dinner, and as close to the heart of Dubrovnik as you can get. With a few tables in the shadow of St Blaise's church and another door in Lučarica, the Penatur is both prominent and intimate, its simple interior of oil paintings and shelves of Pelješac wine housing 40 or so guests. Most opt for fish – fresh and 280kn by the kilo – although decent meaty mains (rib steak, 65kn, veal medallions, 70kn) are also available. Throw in a bottle of Dingač (170kn) or Pošip (140kn) and you've got a satisfying supper.

Poco Loco

Buničeva poljana 5 (020 323 410). **Open** 9am-1am daily. **Bar**. No credit cards. **Map** p49 D4 ③⑤
Not even a little bit mad, but this petite corner bar squeezed in behind the busy terrace of the Troubador invariably has a free spot when it's tourist hell outside. A steady soundtrack of pop and dance favourites chivvies the atmosphere along but you do get the feeling that the barman has had enough and wouldn't mind going home soon.

Poklisar

Ribarnica 1 (020 322 176). **Open** 8am-midnight daily. **Restaurant**. **Map** p49 E3 ③⑥
With its twin terraces occupying both sides of a prominent square overlooking the old harbour, the Poklisar cannot fail to buzz in high season. The prices, given the location, are reasonable – pizzas at 45kn, sea fish of the day at 230kn for two people, even grilled lobster is 430kn a kilo, astronomical elsewhere. Among the standard choices are shrimps in saffron sauce or home-made gnocchi with

Taverna Arsenal p71

gorgonzola and rocket, and desserts deserve a detour once you step off the boat back from Lokrum: walnut pancakes, hazelnut or wild fruit parfaits. Get here before the cheesy live music drowns out the lovely lap of the sea.

Proto

Široka 1 (020 323 234). **Open** 11am-11pm daily. **Restaurant**. **Map** p48 C3 ③⑦
From the same family as the upmarket Nautika (p95), the fish-oriented Proto cannot fail to be classy. As well as mussels, squid and lobster in simple but superbly balanced sauces, there are more unusual finds from nearby Pelješac, snails for example. The fish soup (48kn) might be the best you'll find in town. An easy option might be to dive in with the fish plate for two (288kn) and spend an enjoyable hour over it. Superb selection of wines, three meal choices for children, regular choice of light lunches – and booking essential. First-floor terrace in summer.

Razonoda

Pucić Palace, Od Puča 1 (020 326 200/ www.thepucicpalace.com). **Open** 11am-midnight daily. **Bar**. **Map** p49 D4 ③⑧
The finest wine bar in town is set in the five-star surroundings of the Pucić Palace. Dalmatian labels comprise the bulk of the extensive selection: Pelješac reds such as an excellent dry Dingač (350kn), a deep Miloš-Plavac (230kn) and a gentle, flowery Grgić (550kn); a Pošip white (280kn) from Korčula or Vugava (260kn) from Vis. Istrian and Slavonian selections feature heavily too. Local *pršut* ham and cheeses can be ordered, plus pastries and desserts.

Rozarij

Prijeko 2 (020 321 257). **Open** *Summer* 11am-midnight daily. *Winter* 5pm-midnight daily. **Restaurant**. **Map** p49 D2 ③⑨
Despite the address on Prijeko, a thoroughfare of tourist-trap eateries, this one is set apart – literally. On a little corner by the junction with Zlatarska, Rozarij offers a slightly higher class of Dalmatian (mainly seafood) specialities in a cosy space decorated with colour photos of Dubrovnik and seafaring topics. There are tables outside too. Most of all, you don't come away feeling that some smarmy restaurateur has just picked your pocket.

DUBROVNIK BY AREA

Market forces

The oldest market in Dubrovnik is located in the prominent, baroque square of **Gundulićeva poljana** (p74), by the Rector's Palace and Cathedral. Centrepiecing the stalls is a statue of 17th-century poet Ivan Gundulić. A market has been set up here since 1892, after the abolition of the Ragusa republic, which did not approve of such things. Traditionally it has been focused on fruit and vegetables, something locals call a Zelena placa, or green market.

The vendors come mainly from the eastern villages of Župa and Konavle outside Dubrovnik, some from the more distant Primorje area. Until the 1980s, the market was spread across the whole square but its size reduced with the decrease in residents and increase in rents. It is difficult to tell whether rapid gentrification here will make Zelena placa a fashionable place to buy food. It certainly is most expensive of the markets in town. A short stroll away by the old harbour, a modest fish market also does good trade.

Saturday is the *spenza*, the weekly shop. Try and get here early. In summer, as well as fruit and vegetables, traders offer seasonal cheese, olives, honey and Mediterranean spices. Some sell home-made loza and travarica, strong flavoured brandy, the type you can't buy elsewhere. In one corner, by the Rector's Palace, stalls sell lavender and cantarion oils, ideal for aroma therapy, and sachets of dried flowers.

Every day at noon a ritual takes place as stallholders approach the last working hour. Watched by equally punctual, attentive cats, an official brings a bucket of corn to feed the pigeons sat patiently on the nearby roofs. Suddenly, scores of birds fill the sky. This is the signal for locals to slope off slowly and congregate over coffee at one of the many terrace cafés.

Surf & Turf

Žudioska (095 817 3578 mobile/098 944 9318 mobile). **Open** *Summer* 11am-midnight daily. **Restaurant**. **Map** p49 D3 🟠

Run by the same people responsible for the wonderful Wanda (p72) nearby, this intimate eaterie brings a touch of finery to the surf and turf genre. Ambitious appetisers (50kn-65kn) include ahi tuna tartare, clams positano and *moules marinières*, while the sandwiches (50kn-60kn: prime beef burger; filet mignon; buffalo mozzarella and tomato), all served with proper potato salad, make for a satisfying lunch. Grilled mains (70kn-100kn), complemented by garlic roasted potatoes and sautéed spinach, include New Zealand lamb chops and thick langoustines. Meats come with brandy or steak sauce, fish with *ponzu wasabi* or salsa – few Old Town venues think beyond the provision of salt and pepper. Save your holiday blow-out for the house special (185kn) of grilled filet mignon and shrimp. Great wines too.

Taj Mahal

Nikole Gučetića 2 (020 323 221). **Open** 9am-11pm daily. **Restaurant**. No credit cards. **Map** p48 C3 🟠

Don't let the name fool you – this is not an Indian restaurant but a Bosnian one, and rather good. The cuisine of landlocked Bosnia is meaty, with fine use of vegetables (particularly peppers) and cheeses. Thus the Taj Mahal special is a veal with mushrooms in a crispy shell, the vegetarian plate is laden with peppers and the recommended starter is fried peppers stuffed with *kajmak*, Bosnian cream cheese. Traditional Turkish-style baklava and thick, black Bosnian coffee round off a satisfying, exotic meal.

Talir

Antuninska 5 (020 323 293/www.talir-dubrovnik.hr). **Open** noon-1am daily. **Bar**. No credit cards. **Map** p48 C2 🟠

Classic actors' bar in the Old Town. Diagonally opposite the gallery of the same name, the Talir has been the scene of many a good time since opening in 1983 – just look at the snapshots on the walls. You're just as likely to rub shoulders with the unpretentious party crowd as any local theatre star, as the Talir has a constant buzz and bonhomie about it. The compact interior is packed on summer nights, drinkers blocking the stepped passageway outside (that's Vaclav Havel doing likewise on the website), so get here early and find a seat.

Taverna Arsenal

Pred Dvorom 1 (020 321 065/www. mea-culpa.hr). **Open** 10am-1am daily. **Bar-restaurant**. **Map** p49 D3 🟠

Mea Culpa, which runs graDskavana (p64) in the same building, transformed this medieval weaponry into a tidy, modern tavern in 2005, its terrace overlooking the old harbour. A spacious vaulted interior containing frames of traditional Dalmatian ships is neatly divided between diners and wine drinkers. Some 40 mainly local wines come 16 by the glass, with plenty of flavoured brandies. Fresh, grilled fish is 300kn a kilo and fillets of swordfish are 110kn amid the top-notch versions of ubiquitous standards. You can equally call up a T-bone steak (140kn) or rumpsteak salad (70kn). A band keeps everyone in a party mood past midnight on Saturdays.

Toni

Nikole Božidarevića 14 (020 323 134). **Open** noon-11pm daily. **Restaurant**. **Map** p48 C3 🟠

Everybody's favourite pasta restaurant in the Old Town – not that Toni does anything spectacular, just turns out a huge variety of shapes and sauces to a budget-conscious clientele. Officially it's a spaghetteria but there are bruschettas and soups too, should a hot, filling bowl of steaming pasta be too much for a summer lunchtime.

Troubador

Bunićeva poljana 2 (020 323 476). **Open** *Summer* 9am-3am daily. *Winter* 5-11pm daily. **Bar**. No credit cards. **Map** p49 D4 🟠

The most famous bar in Dalmatia now looks like a billboard for T-Mobile, and if you didn't know that this was the lovely old Troubador, you wouldn't touch it with a bargepole. But lovely old Troubador it is, and visit it you must. Run by Marco, a member of renowned 1960s group the Dubrovački Trubadori, it was a touchstone for artists, musicians and entertainers of his golden generation. These days it's a money-making machine. In summer, the terrace is given over to free jazz concerts and waiters rush between tables packed with tourists. Inside is now only a tiny room of three tables, an atmospheric back area long sold off. Cocktails (50kn-60kn) and sandwiches (15kn-20kn) are also available.

Wanda

Prijeko 8 (098 944 9317 mobile/ 098 944 9318 mobile/www.wanda restaurant.com). **Open** *Apr-Nov* 10.30am-1am daily. Closed Dec-Mar. **Restaurant**. **Map** p49 D2 ㊶

The big success of 2006 has breathed new life into Prijeko, until recently a tourist trap rat run of shamelessly average restaurants. Top Med cuisine at reasonable prices. See box p66.

Shopping

Algebra

Stradun 9 (020 323 217). **Open** 9.30am-7pm Mon-Sat. **Map** p49 D3 ❶

Among the shelves of local-language publications, this prominent little souvenir and bookshop has a reasonable selection of books about Dubrovnik, Dalmatia, Croatia and the Balkans in English. You can also find bags and tablecloths handmade with special embroidery from local villages.

Algoritam

Stradun 8 (020 322 044/www. algoritam.hr). **Open** 9am-8.30pm Mon-Fri; 9am-3pm Sat; 10am-1pm Sun. **Map** p49 D3 ❷

If you've lost, forgotten or galloped through your holiday reads quicker than anticipated, this bookshop is a boon. Half the store is dedicated to English-language publications: from travel guides to bestsellers, classics to heavyweight volumes on politics, history, art and design. Also has an impressive stock of two dozen (pricy) English magazines (*Q, Arena, Vogue*), postcards, CDs and glossy photographic album histories of Dubrovnik.

Aquarius

Poljana Paška Miličevića 4 (020 323 388). **Open** 9am-7.30pm Mon-Sat; 9am-1pm Sun. **Map** p48 B2 ❸

Part of the Aquarius chain, with its own record label, this is the best one-stop shop for music. Located near the Pile Gate, Aquarius carries the latest UK and US music releases as well as a comprehensive selection of releases by Croatian rock, pop and jazz artists. There is a folk section too, with examples of traditional Dalmatian *klapa*, and a good classical offering.

Art Studio Trabakul

Zlatarska 1 (098 851 477 mobile). **Open** 9.30am-6pm Mon-Fri; 9.30am-2.30pm Sat. **Map** p49 D3 ❹

Down near the old harbour, AST is set in a scaled down replica of a Trabakul, the wooden ship of the Adriatic. This ship shop is packed with even smaller ceramic, wood and fabric replica boats manned by charmingly rough pottery fishermen – some stare, some work, others swig bottles. There are also old photographs of Dubrovnik, the most interesting postcards on the market. Pleasantly free of tacky souvenirs.

Croata

Pred Dvorom 2 (020 323 526/www.croata.hr). **Open** 9.30am-7pm Mon-Fri; 9.30am-1.30pm Sat. **Map** p49 D4 ❺

Britain has the bowler, France has the beret and Bavaria the comedy leather trousers. And Croatia? Croatia has the cravat. Croatia is the home of the cravat. It's the national cultural symbol. Even the word 'cravat' comes from the Croatian word for 'Croat': *hrvat*. Not surprisingly, Croatia takes this tradition seriously. It even boasts an academic institution to research the heritage of the necktie. This store is the flagship Dubrovnik branch of the prestigious fashion house chain, selling the kind of garments they always offer to passing dignitaries, men and women. Shawls, scarves and purses too.

Djardin

Miha Pracata 8 (020 324 744). **Open** 9.30am-6pm Mon-Fri; 9.30am-12.30pm Sat. **Map** p48 C3 ❻

This may be easier to find if you look for its entrance on Od Puča. For sheer quantity, this seemingly never-ending tardis of a shop has rooms leading to further rooms leading to courtyards all

Art Studio Trabakul p73

draped with necklaces, rings and the like. There's also a lot of shop assistants and it feels a bit like a glamorous jewellery superstore, but you're bound to find something you like.

Dubrovačka kuća

Od sv Dominika (020 322 092). **Open** 9am-9.30pm Mon-Sat; 9am-7.30pm Sun. **Map** p49 E2 **7**

A great range of high quality souvenirs from local liquors and sweets to art books and posters. There are also olive oil, regional wines, products made from truffle oil, bath salts, ties and dolls. The real jewel is their collaboration with the Museum of Arts and Crafts in Zagreb to create the Museum Shop: a floor full of great ceramics, crockery and glassware; beautiful pieces at affordable prices. Look out for fine plates by Dubravka Rakoći, Bane Milenković, Damir Sokić and Nina Ivančić.

Eminence Art Workshop

Kunićeva 4 (no phone). **Open** 10am-10pm daily. **Map** p48 C2 **8**

At this tasteful craft and souvenir store, the titular Emin makes most of the work himself, sat behind a battered desk. The souvenirs here are a cut above – carved wooden female faces, some with old rope for hair, African in style but with a Mediterranean feel. The going rate is a hefty 3,000kn-4,000kn but jewellery and quirky, colourful hand-painted wooden fish (150kn) – crying out to be placed on a kid's bedroom wall – go for much less. There's also an impressive collection of work by the renowned Croatian artist Zvonimir Keček whose modern take on Orthodox iconography is well worth further investigation.

Franciscan Monastery Pharmacy

Stradun 2 (020 321 411). **Open** 8am-noon Mon-Sat. **Map** p48 B2 **9**

The most remarkable thing about coming here is that locals have been doing the same for nearly 700 years – from 1317 in fact. Part of the Franciscan Monastery complex (p53), the oldest

working pharmacy in Europe offers home-produced cosmetics and medicines. Some of the products are based on the recipes dating from the 14th century and made from the local herbs and plant extracts. Marvel at the beautiful old vases and containers while they wrap your purchase for you.

Franja Coffee & Teahouse

Od Puča 9 (020 324 816). **Open** 9am-7pm Mon-Sat. **Map** p48 B3 **10**

The finest delicatessen in town, Franja does not just stock the finest regional coffees, imported teas and flavoured local ones, but also the best goods Croatia can produce: wines, virgin olive oils, nuts in honey, cheeses in oil and home-made jams. Wines, liqueurs and fruit brandies are another of Franja's specialities, sparkling wines, chocolates and bonbons too. This shop is Franja's third direct-to-customer outlet, the other two being in Zagreb. They also offer gift packages.

Gundulićeva poljana market

Gundulićeva poljana (no phone). **Open** 6am-1pm Mon-Sat. **Map** p49 D4 **11**

One of the pleasures of the Old Town is the fact that there is a regular local fruit and vegetable market right by the main square. Prices here are more expensive than at the one near the ferry terminal at Gruž, but this is the ideal place to pick up a bag of goodies to take to the beach. P70 **Market forces**.

Ivana Bačura

Zlatarska 3 (091 543 1321 mobile/ www.ivanabacura.com). **Open** 9.30am-6.30pm Mon-Fri; 9.30am-12.30pm Sat. **Map** p49 D3 **12**

This Zagreb-based designer offers something more contemporary and personal than other venues in town – every one of Ivana's pieces is handmade. Her jewellery is stylish, simple and quite often silver. Bačura's use of stone is calm – all muted reds, greens and blues – and her rings and earrings are nicely understated. What's here is original enough to impress without being overbearing.

New store for urban style

Welcome to Croatia's leading streetwear boutique.

Eminence Art Workshop p74

It's not only restaurateurs and gallery owners who are challenging staid old Stari Grad – it's clothes shops too. The opening of Sheriff & Cherry's local outlet in the Old Town in April 2007 can be seen as a landmark move if this museum city is going to move away from tacky tourism and somewhere closer to the 21st century.

Sheriff & Cherry (p77) is the brainchild of Rovinj-born Mauro, whose set up his first store in his home town in Istria. Responsible for a fashion consultancy in Barcelona, Mauro was keen to break down barriers back in Croatia. Always the most forward-thinking and open-minded region of Croatia, close to the Italian border, Istria took to his edgy fashion store like a duck to water. Summer trade boomed, the many Italian visitors to this gay-friendly resort delighted to find clothes and shoes and accessories by labels such as Paul & Joe, Juan

Antonio López and Jordi Labanda. The store was striking, imaginative and changed its decor every two months. Another was opened in Zagreb, stocking Y-3, Schwipe, Trainerspotter and Nudie. The basement is filled with limited edition adidas hats and caps.

Dalmatia came next. 'Dubrovnik is hard because space is so limited,' said Mauro, explaining his decision to open an outlet of only 32sq m. 'Rent and rates are high. Easy access for deliveries is tricky.' Realising that tastes here were more traditional, Mauro gave the store a maritime feel, stocking bags, shoes and accessories to tailor to summer demand.

Most of S&C's stock is foreign-branded. 'Croatian designers still lack the nous of those in Spain or London,' said Mauro. 'I like I-GLE, Zagreb designers Martina Vrdoljak Ranilović and Nataša Mihaljčišin. Trends move slowly here. It's time we started to push ahead.'

jegerStar

Od Puča 7 (020 323 847/www.jeger star.com). Open 8am-8.30pm Mon-Fri; 9am-2pm Sat. Map p48 B3 ⓭

The most established store in town for urban fashion, featured every other month in the Croatian edition of *Cosmopolitan*, jegerStar carries global brands such as Diesel, Kicker, Irregular Choice, Camper and Nautica. The price tags are hefty compared to what you can find in London if you shop around – but the upscale, young professional clientele don't seem to mind.

Kadena

Celestina Medovića 2 (no phone). Open 9am-8pm daily. Map p48 B2 ⓮

Located down the first street on the left as you enter the Old Town through the Pile Gate, this small, friendly women's shop stocks only Croatian designers. One particularly worth checking out is Nebo. It's not haute couture but neither are the prices – there are hats for 90kn, blouses 350kn, coats and dresses 990kn. There's a distinctive 1960s style in both cut and prints, and there are items that you wouldn't find easily elsewhere. Kadena also carries some

Ivana Bačura p74

interesting jewellery made by the young Croatian designer Dado Zorica.

Kraš Bonbonnière

Zamanjina 2 (020 321 049/www.kras. hr). Open 9am-7pm Mon-Sat. Map p49 D3 ⓯

Approaching its centenary, one of the most famous brands in Croatia was renamed after an anti-fascist hero from World War II, Josip Kraš. The confectionery makers have since branched out from bonbons to produce wafers, tea biscuits, powders, sprinkles and cooking chocolates. Pride of place goes to Kraš' Bajaderas, sweets of exquisite almond-enriched almonds, all individually wrapped and oriental in flavour. Griottes have sour-cherry centres in dark chocolate coating. There are selection and souvenir boxes too. Ideal gifts but you may be tempted to dip in.

Lobel Galerija

Od Domina 1 (020 324 940/098 706 706 mobile/www.lobelgalerija.com). Open 9am-8pm Mon-Fri; 9am-7pm Sat. Map p48 B3 ⓰

The trendiest place for furniture and homeware, established by local design graduate Martina Kortizija Franić. For moneyed, style-conscious long-term expat residents, this equally fashionable two-floor boutique should be your one-stop shop for domestic comfort. Advice on interior design is all part of the service. Lobel also carries easy, chic items to take back to the UK too, such as glassware, and bronze and crystal articles by Baldi of Venice, or ceramics by Treviso's New Trend.

Lush

Široka 4 (020 324 797/www.lush.com). Open 9am-9pm Mon-Sat; 10am-6pm Sun. Map p48 C3 ⓱

All the foxy, fragrant and ethical products of this Poole-based cosmetics company are available here in Dubrovnik. Fresh, hand-made soaps, body butters, shampoos, bath bombs and perfumes, none produced by means of animal testing, give out a distinctive aroma as you turn into Široka from Stradun.

Opening in April 2007, the urban style store Sheriff & Cherry will give staid old dame Dubrovnik just that little missing element of street credibility. See box p75.

Trinity

Palmotićeva 2 (020 322 350/www. trinity.hr). **Open** 9.30am-6.30pm Mon-Fri; 9.30am-noon Sat. **Map** p48 C2 ⑳
The best place in town for a necklace, with an almost unlimited selection of shapes, sizes and colours beautifully arranged across an equally beautiful two-floor space, to be three floors by the summer of 2007. Opening hours may also be extended. You'll find pearls, corals and jade, both chunky and delicate. A cut above its many competitors and with prices to match.

Turbo limač

Zamanjina 1 (020 321 193/www.turbo limac.com). **Open** 9am-8.30pm Mon-Fri; 9am-2pm Sat. **Map** p48 C3 ㉑
On the corner of Zamanjina and Stradun, Turbo limač stocks everything for the little ones – toys and games (including Lego, Power Rangers and Transformers), dolls, costumes, clothes, sports goods, rucksacks, even prams and furniture. Most of the goods on offer are of the branded, Western variety, and not cheap by any means.

Vinoteka Dubrovnik

Stradun (020 321 777/098 748 868 mobile/www.mali-podrum.com). **Open** 10am-8pm daily. **Map** p48 C3 ㉒
Halfway along Stradun, this small, friendly shop contains a reasonable selection of local and international wines. A comprehensive list of the domestic varieties on offer in-store or by order is on the website. For a standard bottle to take to the beach, you'll find cheaper at one of the local groceries outside the Pile Gate. For the quality take-home labels – a 1999 Dingač Plavac-Mali by Vina Miličić, for example, or a 1990 one by Badel 1862 – you need go no further. Vinoteka also stocks olive oils and strong, clear regional spirits in a range of fruit, nut and even mistletoe flavours.

Ronchi

Lučarica 2 (020 323 699). **Open** 9am-noon, 4-7pm Mon-Fri; 9am-noon Sat. **Map** p49 D3 ⑱
Ronchi is a Dubrovnik institution. In business since 1858, this landmark family-run women's hat shop is nowadays in the capable hands of English-speaking Marina Ronchi Grabovac. This personable milliner still uses the same techniques passed down the generations for designing and making beautiful and unusual creations. Ronchi Grabovac's straw varieties are always a hit in summer, while other patterns borrow from local folk and late 19th-century influences. Grabovac also has a selection of gentlemen's hats, equally suited to summer wear.

Sheriff & Cherry

Djordićeva 4 (www.sheriffandcherry. com). **Open** 10am-2pm, 5-10pm Mon-Fri; 10am-2pm Sat. **Map** p48 C3 ⑲

Nightlife

Labirint

Sv Dominika (020 322 222/www.labirint-dubrovnik.com). **Open** *Summer* 10pm-5am daily. **Map** p49 E2 **①**

The post-midnight element of the Labirint complex reopened in 2005 after a lengthy refurbishment. As in the case of the restaurant (p67), the setting is perfect, overlooking the old harbour from the Sv Luka battlement, and the spot opposite the Dominican monastery conveniently close. Unsurprisingly, though, Labirint offers a tacky, mainstream after-hours experience. It's not jacket-and-tie, but it's an undemanding, moneyed clientele who open their collar buttons and make the shift from restaurant table to basement bar and disco. The agenda for 2006 involved ladies' nights on Fridays and karaoke on Saturdays – the recently installed father-and-son Russian management (yikes!) may be making a few changes before the 2007 season starts.

Arts & leisure

Artur Gallery

Lučarica 1 (020 420 305/020 423 744). **Open** 9am-1pm, 5-7pm Mon-Fri. **Map** p49 D3 **①**

This little gallery puts on regular exhibitions by local artists, as well as art workshops. The gift shop sells tasteful souvenirs, jewellery and albums related to Dubrovnik. Look out for books by Italian cartoonist Osvaldo Cavandolli. His drawings found inspiration in Dubrovnik thanks to gallery owner Tea Batinić, who invited him here a few years ago. The result was *Dubrovnik*, 35 stories written by Batinić, illustrated by Cavandolli.

Carmel Photo Gallery

Zamanjina 10 (020 320 222/www.photogallerycarmel.com). **Open** *Jan-May* 10am-1pm, 5-8pm Tue-Sat. *June-Dec* 9am-9pm daily. **Map** p49 D3 **②**

Surrounded by bars and restaurants, this solitary bastion of fine-art photography emerged in 2006. The gallery

offers diverse exhibitions of regional and international photographers, either young talents or stalwart professionals. Founder Erik Walker, from Carmel, California, encourages the inclusion of compatriots such as Edward Weston, Ansel Adams and John Sexton. Most exhibitions are solo shows lasting one month, with the works available for purchase. In high season the programme focuses on the photography of Dubrovnik and area.

Dulčić, Masle, Pulitika Gallery

Poljana Marina Držića 1 (020 323 172). **Open** 10am-8pm Tue-Sun. **Admission** *including entry to the Museum of Modern Art* 30kn; free concessions. No credit cards. **Map** p49 D4 **③**

While the Museum of Modern Art (p84) focuses on the new and the global, its sister operation the DMP named after renowned modern artists concentrates

Dulčić, Masle, Pulitika Gallery

Quality art for sale

Dubrovnik is awash with bad art and tacky souvenirs. The best place in the Old Town to buy (and see) high-quality, contemporary Croatian art is **Galerija Sebastian** (p80). Opened in 1972, the gallery's name derives from its location in the former Church of St Sebastian. The portfolio of work on offer is extensive and varied, originals and limited prints. These days it concentrates on Croatian artists as opposed to those from across former Yugoslavia.

The Sebastian is owned and managed by knowledgeable Jadranka Nikolić, who admits that the bulk of her customers are tourists. 'Nowadays Croatians tend to be very rich or very poor. The middle class disappeared in the war. The teachers, professors and doctors who used to buy art today can't afford to. Those that can afford it often buy direct from the artists' ateliers rather than from a gallery.'

Jadranka concentrates on and excels in contemporary art that uses traditional media: paintings, sculptures and drawings.

'Installations are great but I guess not many tourists will buy an installation,' she says. Jadranka works with more than 50 artists including Croatian representatives at the Venice Biennale. She describes it as 'a wide range of styles but the best of the best'.

Exhibitions here change rapidly, a new one every three weeks. This enables her to showcase some six to eight artists every year. One to look out for in 2007 is Dubravka Lošić, once voted the world's best young artist at the Grand Palais in Paris. Lošić will be hosting her third exhibition in this 90-sq m exhibition space, high-ceilinged and flooded by great natural light.

Prices can reach up to 60,000kn (€8,000) for a painting by naive artist Ivan Rabuzin but you can also find something for as little as 400kn (€54). Ana Zanze's lovely collages and pencil drawings on the backs of postcards sell for 1,000kn (€135). You can also pick up limited edition prints (runs of 120) by the recently deceased and much missed Lipovac for 2,400kn (€325).

on important figures from the last 200 years. The two-storey gallery owns more than 2,200 pieces but only a fraction are on show. On the top floor, the most important artist is well represented: Vlaho Bukovac. His landscapes are of value but it's his portraits that shine, often with a definite melancholic, contemplative edge. Pieces by contemporary local artists, brasher and brighter, are downstairs.

Galerija Sebastian

Sv Dominika 5 (020 321 490). **Open** *Apr-Sept* 9am-9pm daily. **Map** p48 E2 ❹
A handy spot in town to view and to buy decent contemporary Croatian art. See box p79.

Jadran cinema

Iza Roka (020 321 425/www.kinema tografi.org). **Open** See programme. No credit cards. **Map** p48 B3 ❺
Open-air cinemas here start up in June and wind down by September. The programme, of course, depends on the weather, but you can count on regular showings of subtitled Croatian and recent international films through July and August. Here at the long established Jadran in the heart of the Old Town, the setting is atmospheric, and quaint to the point of antiquated, from the projecting equipment to the 300 old wooden seats. Cinema staff hand out cushions to visitors as they enter. Screenings take place in the early evening, allowing filmgoers to take advantage of the city-centre location right after the show.

Lero Theatre

Ilije Sarake 7 (020 324 051). **Map** p49 D5 ❻
The Student Theatre Lero, as this amateur company is affectionately known, was founded in the political turbulence of 1968. The group acquired an almost legendary status in the alternative art scene and picked up numerous awards. The Lero only stages one show a year. Recent productions have included works by Bertolt Brecht, Eugène Ionesco, the Russian avant-garde and modern interpretations of Ragusan classics. The Lero doesn't have its own stage and usually performs on the Bursa stage of Marin Držić (see below).

Marin Držić Theatre

Pred Dvorom 3 (www.kazaliste-dubrovnik.hr). Office *Kovačka 1 (020 321 006).* **Open** according to programme. No credit cards. **Map** p49 D4 ❼
The only existing theatre in the city, named after Dubrovnik's most renowned playwright, the Marin Držić was installed where the old Town Hall stands. This privately built neo-Renaissance edifice, with an ornate interior, opened its doors to the public in 1865. Although the auditorium is rather small, it has staged many extraordinary performances. Marin Držić is a repertory theatre with a permanent company, whose programme is based on the literary heritage of Dubrovnik, as well as national and international classics. The venue is central to the annual Dubrovnik Festival.

Sloboda cinema

Luža (020 321 425/www.kinema tografi.org). **Open** according to programme. No credit cards. **Map** p49 D3 ❽
Although it's right in the main square, and the only year-round cinema in town, the 'Freedom' cinema is easily passed by. It is located on the first floor of a former local authority building, whose elaborate baroque portal is set next to the clock tower. Look out for the posters. The auditorium, decorated in contemporary style, is large enough to contain nearly 300 seats, screens daily showings Croatian and international releases. All films are subtitled.

War Photo Limited

Antuninska 6 (020 322 166/www.war photoltd.com). **Open** *May-Oct* 9am-9pm daily. *Nov, Dec, Mar, Apr* 10am-4pm Tue-Sat; 10am-2pm Sun. Closed Jan, Feb. **Admission** 25kn. **Map** p48 C2 ❾
Conflict around the globe seen through the eyes of leading photo-journalists. See box p56.

Ploče

Ploče is the picturesque stretch of coastline and sliver of land running east from the gate of the same name towards the resorts of Župa Dubrovačka and Cavtat, and Dubrovnik airport.

Until relatively recently, coast and land were pretty much all that were here. Traders would bring their wares over the hillsides by donkey to the Old Town and set up on the open ground outside the **Ploče Gate**. The view of **Lokrum island**, which lounges the length of Ploče, was enjoyed by passing peasants from Konavle and Bosnia and the handful of nobles who built isolated villas overlooking the sea.

The modest rows of residential housing here, separated by steep-stepped narrow streets connecting the three main roads, Jadranska cesta, Kralja Petra Krešimira and Frana Supila, rose at the same time as the lure of tourism encouraged villa owners to convert their homes.

Away from the five-star hotels – the **Excelsior** (and Villa Odak), the **Grand Villa Argentina**, **Villa Dubrovnik** – and their restaurants, today there isn't much social life to connect with. The only exception is immediately around the Ploče Gate. Often overlooked, the **Museum of Modern Art** is worth the short trek from the Old Town. Diagonally opposite, the old quarantine barracks of **Lazareti** is the town's major DJ club, a live venue, art gallery and shop in one. Look out for one-off DJ events at the **Belvedere**, a ruined congress hotel overlooking Ploče's most popular beach, **Sv Jakov**. Back near the Old Town, the **Revelin Fort** is also used for DJ nights.

Brave new world

The Museum of Modern Art showcases novel creations

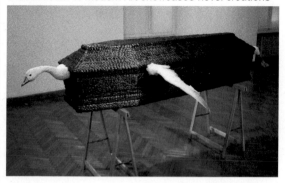

The Banac Mansion would be an attraction in itself. Built in the 1930s for the wealthy local ship owner of the same name, it was converted in 1950 to house this superb collection of mainly 20th-century Croatian art. The aim of the **Museum of Modern Art** (p84) is to 'make Dubrovnik once again a metropolis, an art centre beyond the local context'. Four floors, nine rooms, some 2,000 square metres of exhibition space inside and out, expansive terraces looking out onto the Adriatic and a garden, combine in this goal. Yet most visitors to Dubrovnik don't even know the museum exists.

Just a few minutes out of the Old Town towards the luxury hotels, you walk into an atrium that seems perfectly suited for installations – which is what it's used for. Other rooms are set up for audio-visual work. The size, scale and natural light work to give a fine ambience for contemplation – a welcome gift of Dubrovnik quiet time, even in high season.

Then again, if you ever wanted a place for a party in Dubrovnik, the huge balcony on the third floor would be it. If there's an opening on while you're here, get invited.

The permanent collection has some 2,000 items; paintings, drawings and sculpture. Not all are on show at the same time. The selection of pieces by Vlaho Bukovac, in particular his portraits, a stand-out of any visit, is rotated.

Temporary exhibitions are held year-round. The highlight of 2006 was a showcase of Jan Fabre, the Belgian installation artist, sculptor and performer, who fully exploited the possibilities the museum space offered. The curator's choices tend to be interesting and challenging, far from the safety of naive art.

This is the only space in town to see such work – nowhere else can cope with the scale. Maybe nowhere else has the remit or the desire; Dubrovnik is a city so focused on its past, it risks neglecting the future.

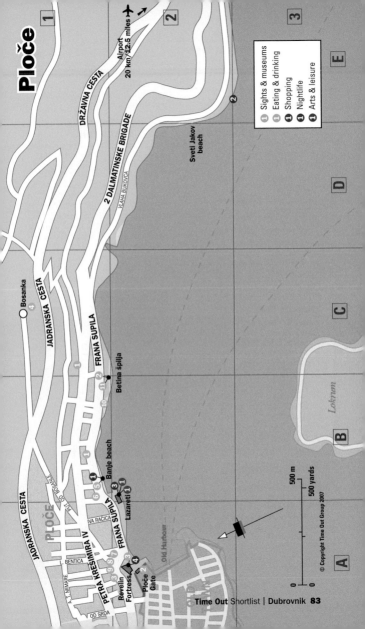

Ploče

Airport
20 km / 12.5 miles

Bosanka ○ ④

JADRANSKA CESTA

DRŽAVNA CESTA

2 DALMATINSKE BRIGADE

VLAHA BUKOVCA

Sveti Jakov beach

Lokrum

FRANA SUPILA

Betina špilja

JADRANSKA CESTA

PLOČE

Banje beach

FRANA SUPILA

Lazareti

PETRA KREŠIMIRA IV

A. T. MIMARE

BENTICA

IVA RAČICA

Reveln

Fortress

Ploče
Gate

Old Harbour

OD SRĐA

500 m

500 yards

© Copyright Time Out Group 2007

① Sights & museums
② Eating & drinking
③ Shopping
④ Nightlife
⑤ Arts & leisure

A   B   C   D   E

1   2   3

Museum of Modern Art

Frana Supila 23 (020 426 590/www.ug dubrovnik.com). **Open** *10am-8pm Tue-Sun.* **Admission** *including entry to the Dulčić, Masle, Pulitika Gallery 30kn; free concessions. No credit cards.*
Map p83 B1 ❶

Wonderful space, superb collection, an easy, short walk from the Old Town – and yet so rarely visited. Guided tours are available by reservation only. See box p82.

Ploče Gate

Map p83 A2 ❷
Built in similar form to its counterpart at the western entrance to the Old Town, the Pile Gate, Ploče comprises inner and outer gates, connected by a drawbridge. Although it lacks the stature of its opposite number – for most of the last century there was nothing much at Ploče to head for, no tram, bus or job to go to – it does offer fine views of the old harbour at night.

Revelin Fort

Map p83 A2 ❸
When news came of the fall of Constantinople to the Turks in 1453, work began rapidly on fortifying the Old Town. Protecting the harbour was paramount. Guarding it from the north-east, a fort was quickly put up, Revelin. Its current appearance is mainly due to the sturdy design of Antonio Ferramolino in the 1540s; it survived the 1667 earthquake. Today it stages Revelin Club DJ parties (p90) and the Dubrovnik Festival.

Biker's Caffe

Kralja Petra Krešimira 37 (091 764 6919 mobile/098 680 711 mobile/ www.bikers-caffe.com). **Open** *noon-midnight daily.* **Bar.** *No credit cards.*
Map p83 C1 ❶

Ah, Dubrovnik. Just when you think you're in a residential neighbourhood of allotments and exclusive hotels, along comes a bar full of hairy-arsed bikers. Actually, the Libertas chapter are a friendly bunch. Old locals drift in for a beer – where else is there to drink in Ploče? – and sit incongruously against the photographic mementos of Libertas Riders' campaigns, Poreč 2001 and so on. Predictable rock soundtrack and soft porn in the bogs.

La Caravelle Lounge Bar & Restaurant

Grand Villa Argentina, Frana Supila 14 (020 440 555/www.gva.hr). **Open** *9.30am-12.30am daily.*
Bar-restaurant. Map p83 B1 ❷
Another fabulous terrace, with the Old Town hovering, bathed in sunset. La Caravelle is set on the panoramic fourth floor of the main Grand Villa Argentina, its terrace half relaxing lounge bar and half white-tableclothed restaurant. A more business-oriented crowd is accommodated here, so the service is swifter, the atmosphere less recreational. The quality of the fare –

Curse of the cruise ships

Packed streets and poor revenue for a misguided policy.

Cruise ships are today's local topic of conversation in town, bar none. Every day in high season, up to ten of these unmissably huge city-at-sea cruisers descend and dock in Dubrovnik, dwarfing the Old Town. Their horns serve as an unofficial wake-up call. If you're staying at the Excelsior or Grand Villa Argentina, these monsters may interrupt your view – surely a reason why you splashed out there in the first place.

In 2006 the disturbance was almost more destructive. A captain had to take frantic, evasive action when two ships locked anchors. Although he avoided crashing into these exclusive hotels in question, guests were evacuated and the debate intensified.

Cruise ships unload a daily cargo of older tourists by the thousand, camcorders surgically attached. They swarm the Old Town's narrow streets, behind a young tour guide with her arms aloft, barking into an in-the-ear microphone piece. Uncouth is not the word for it. Most whistle-stop tours take two hours. Passengers are instructed not to take too much money with them – as if Dubrovnik is dangerous! – and are encouraged to visit favoured, tacky souvenir shops. A few transitory visitors consume a quick coffee.

Despite the docking fees cruise companies pay the city, Dubrovnik becomes even more oppressively busy in high season and earns an unfair image as a destination for the old. The debate extends further. How should Dubrovnik's future be directed as a tourist destination? Mass or elite? Package or independent traveller?

Bermuda solved the riddle in 2005 by limiting cruise ships to 6,000 passengers a day entering the town. The loss in dock revenue has been offset by an increase in spending per head around town.

The next generation of cruise ships will be 800 feet in length and carry 2,000 passengers each. The question is, can Dubrovnik afford to say no?

Beach fun day and night

East-West on Banje beach

Dubrovnik's city beach, **Banje**, is a short walk from the Ploče Gate. It's good for kids, pebbly and at times sandy, depending on the waves. It has showers, deckchairs and sunloungers for hire, plus jet skis and inflatables. Yet since the city sold half the beach to **East-West** (p88), locals have deserted the place in droves on principle.

They head for **Sveti Jakov**, down the coast past the Villa Dubrovnik, a 20-minute walk along quiet, tree-lined Vlaha Bukovca. Buses nos.5 and 8 run most of the way from north of the Old Town. Although this is everyone's favourite beach, it's rarely crowded. The sun stays warm until late in the evening, bathing the Old Town in a golden light. It's part shingle, part pebble, with showers, sun shades, and a bar and restaurant at beach level. A volleyball court, jet skis and sea kayaks are also to hand.

It is accessed via a long stairway you'll be reluctant to climb back up. Above stands the Benedictine monastery St James of Višnjica, with historic ties to the baroque writer Ignjat Djurdjević. Here, also on the promontory, is the ruined **Hotel Belvedere** (p90), site of the best one-off DJ parties in summer. Sv Jakov is liberal. Naked night dips and bar parties are the norm.

Between Banje and Sv Jacob are the hotel beaches, either exclusive or hired by the day. Each can offer pool, a terrace and a fine Martini. Just east of the Grand Villa Argentina is **Betina špilja**, a cave with a fine white pebble beach, only accessible from the sea. Rent a taxi boat at the old harbour, arrange a pick-up time and get the captain's number. Take provisions with you. The more adventurous can swim 100 metres from the beach at the Villa Sheherezade in the hotel complex. Above the cave is the Getaldić mansion. The 16th-century mathematician Marin Getaldić practised experiments below – one of his mirrors is in the Maritime Museum in Greenwich.

Dalmatian and international classics, finely concocted and equally finely presented – doesn't suffer, all the same. Cocktails on the terrace provide the perfect finale to the night if you're staying around this side of town.

Chihuahua – Cantina Mexicana

Hvarska 6 (020 424 445). **Open** 5-11pm daily. **Restaurant**. No credit cards. **Map** p83 A2 ③

A free-standing house in a prime spot over the north wall of the Old Town, this friendly yellow-painted eaterie serves up a mess of Mexican food. For the price (enchiladas, tacos, fajitas and burritos in the 50kn range), it's an easy option. The house special (90kn) of grilled turkey, steak and spare ribs requires dedication, as do the barbecue-meat grills (55kn-79kn). Bottles of Desperados and Corona, shots of Sauza or Olmeca tequila, sangria 80kn a litre. A couple of tables are set outside.

Dubrava

Bosanka (020 416 405/098 162 4182 mobile). **Open** *Summer* noon-midnight daily. *Winter* varies. **Restaurant**. No credit cards. **Map** p83 C1 ④

The village of Bosanka stands some 200 metres above Ploče on a hilly slope of Mount Srdj. Outside the village on the Ploče side stands this traditional stone restaurant, recommended by locals. Spit-roasted lamb and game are the house specialities, but phone ahead and see what the chef wished prepare that day *ispod peke*, slow-braised under a cooking bell covered in hot coals. Always check opening hours in winter. An irregular city bus now runs to Bosanka – but it's probably a taxi job.

East-West

Banje beach/Frana Supila (020 412 220/020 312 573/098 981 3851 mobile/www.ew-dubrovnik.com). **Open** 9.30am-12.30am. **Bar-restaurant**. **Map** p83 B1 ⑤

Restaurant, bar and club complex in one, with its own private half of what was the public beach, shamelessly sold off by the city. East-West is a tidy oper-ation all the same. Its dining element is upscale and somewhat formal. Salmon and marinated aubergine (60kn) or prawns on rocket (80kn) feature as starters, pastas (60kn-70kn) may come with truffles and mushrooms, or caviar or vodka. The fishermen's salad (48kn) with anchovies, rocket and fusilli is a winner, breaded skate (65kn) a nice find among the fish. The extensive wine list includes 30 varieties (Radović Dingač or Grgić Pošip the stand-outs at 290kn), four by the half-bottle.

Konoba Pjatanca

Koločepska 2 (020 420 949). **Open** *Mar-Oct* 9am-midnight daily. Closed Nov-Feb. **Restaurant**. No credit cards. **Map** p83 B1 ⑥

A cut above the average *konoba*, not least because of its roofed terrace and sea view, just set back from the main road. The food, too, is superior home cooking at standard prices, significantly below what you would pay in the Old Town, not even ten minutes' walk away. Grilled meats, squid, catch of the day, appropriately and simply garnished with fresh salad or *blitva*. A handy everyday bolthole to know in this locality of luxury hospitality.

Laura

Frana Supila 1 (098 428 278 mobile). **Open** 7am-2am daily. **Bar**. No credit cards. **Map** p83 B2 ⑦

Ever wandered around the Old Town and wished there was a corner bar just for locals, in which everyone was a bit pissed up in a fun way, and where the music was half-decent? Welcome to Laura. Occupying a strategic corner by the Ploče Gate, with a right-angle of tables outside for perfect sundowners, Laura buzzes from breakfast (45kn) to way past the witching hour. If there's no sport on the big TV screen, they'll put on either well-chosen electronica or guitar-driven sounds. Attracts an older clientele but you wouldn't call it staid.

Maestoso

Put od Bosanke 4 (020 420 986). **Open** 10am-midnight daily. **Restaurant**. **Map** p83 A2 ⑧

A traditional terrace restaurant at the corner of Hvarska and Frana Supila overlooking the Ploče Gate, Maestoso charges Old Town prices for ambitious Dalmatian cuisine. Grilled lobster is a standard main (170kn, 255kn for two), and rocket features in most of the ten salads. Not everything works – should oysters be breaded? Is this the place for French onion soup? – but at least you're not struggling with another samey menu. An alfresco lunch of the house cold platter (air-dried ham, octopus, cheese, 90kn) should hit the spot. Half-a-dozen decent domestic wines by the glass, 15 by the bottle.

Tabasco Pizzeria

Hvarska 48A (020 429 595). **Open** *Summer* 10am-midnight daily. *Winter* varies. **Restaurant**. **Map** p83 A1 ❾

Standard pizzeria, far enough away from the madding Old Town crowds to be a pleasant, easy, cheap, lunchtime interlude after a morning at nearby Banje beach. By the evening, you'll find better options here around the Ploče Gate. Beware, the *panzerotti* are bloody enormous – you can share with your dining companion. The pizzas, 15 or so, are more modest and thin of crust. There are a handful of pasta dishes too.

Taverna Rustica

Hotel Excelsior, Frana Supila 12 (020 353 353/www.hotel-excelsior.hr). **Open** 5.30pm-12.30am daily. **Restaurant**. **Map** p83 B1 ❿

Like the Hotel Excelsior it occupies, the signposted Taverna Rustica has been decoratively overhauled during the winter of 2006. The chalet feel remains, a musician might still provide subtle acoustic accompaniment to your meal from the balcony – but, most of all, the cuisine is top-five-in-town stellar. You won't find a better lobster bisque (115kn), that's for sure. For a main, the roasted monkfish with turmeric dill sauce (160kn) or baked duck breast filled with porcini mushrooms (165kn) are difficult to overlook, even for local offerings such as the varied seafood platter from the Elafiti islands (600kn).

Sauces can also be ordered, lobster (25kn) or mushroom and truffle (25kn). Service and presentation add to the superb experience.

Victoria Restaurant

Villa Orsula, Grand Villa Argentina, Frana Supila 14 (020 440 555/www.gva.hr). **Open** *Summer* 11am-12.30am daily. *Winter* varies. **Restaurant**. **Map** p83 B1 ⓫

Fine dining in one of the finest small hotels on the Adriatic, the Villa Orsula, the most characteristic of the Grand Villa Argentina complex. A sumptuous, verdant dining terrace offers the perfect view of the Old Town while attentive staff bring forth superior versions of Dalmatian standards, garnished with fresh vegetables done just right. Choose from an extensive wine list or let the waiter do it for you.

Shopping

DEŠA

Lazareti complex, Banje beach, Frana Supila 8 (020 420 145/www.desa-dubrovnik.net/en/center). **Open** 8.30am-4pm Mon-Fri. No credit cards. **Map** p83 B2 ❶

Traditional techniques of weaving, silk embroidery, sewing and craft-making are employed by local women at this workshop and souvenir store in a large downstairs area of the multi-tasked Lazareti complex. You shouldn't just buy out of goodwill – the items on offer are of good quality, colourful and original, a million miles away from the Asian-made toot and trash purveyed as souvenirs in the Old Town.

Nightlife

East-West

Frana Supila (020 412 220/www.ew-dubrovnik.com). **Open** *Summer* 5pm-3am daily. **Map** p83 B1 ❶

Occupying one half of the town's public beach, East-West is a café and restaurant by day and a clubby beach-side cocktail bar by night. The location, right on Banje beach within five minutes of the Old Town, is perfect. The

Watch this space

A new long-term lease is signed for the Lazareti.

'The space is so prominent, they wanted to make it a casino or a row of small shops,' laughs Slaven Tolj, new owner of the **Lazareti** (p90) complex. In 2006, after years of wrangling, this project leader with an ambitious vision of how the Lazareti should serve Dubrovnik secured a 25-year lease on the property. The cluster of historic 16th-century seafront buildings that once made up Dubrovnik's quarantine quarters near the City Walls have been spared commercial development.

The lease includes the adjacent beach too. Tolj has plans for open-air events in summer or, he says, 'we could just enjoy the space'.

Since the 1990s, the Lazareti has filled the considerable gap marked 'youth culture' in the local calendar. Four spaces, 1,000 square metres centrepieced by an open-air courtyard, are run on a multi-disciplinary ethos. Slaven and others have staged concerts, film festivals and exhibitions for a diverse mix of open-minded locals

and tourists in the know. Lazareti stages DJ nights, but the building converts into a live music venue for 500 people, 175 seated.

The long-term acquisition has given Slaven the confidence to expand and 'deliver an exciting ongoing series of events all year round'. While local DJs man the decks at weekends, international names will be encouraged to come in and out of season. 'We want to up the quality of the live music element,' says Slaven. 'We should be able to persuade artists to play in such impressive surroundings.' In 2006 live highlights included the Bambi Molesters, Let 3 and TBF, the best Croatia can offer, DJs Billy Nasty and LTJ Bukem, festivals of film and performing arts, and a link-up with Zagreb underground club, the Močvara.

'We want to be independent, financially and in our decision-making. We want the bar and concerts to pay for our arts projects – not spend all our time chasing grants,' says Slaven.

clientele tends to be pretty glitzy – it's often hired for fashion parties (*Playboy* Croatia, after-party for Best Model in Croatia) – but the place is comfortable rather than intimidating. Prices aren't much different than anywhere else. Thirty-odd cocktails are 50kn each, the drink-this-and-fall-over East-West of vodka, gin, tequila, rum, Triple Sec, Sprite plus energy drink 100kn. A DJ spins unobtrusive music.

Hotel Belvedere

Sv Jakov beach, Vlaha Bukovca (www.clubpages.net). **Open** *Summer according to programme.* No credit cards. **Map** p83 E2 ❷

Quite possibly the best DJ spot on this stretch of the southern Adriatic is this ruined congress hotel out by Sveti Jakov beach at the far end of Ploče. Certainly the three nights organised here by clubpages.net in August 2006 – two by former V2 mixer Ian Pooley, one by Laus Radio featuring local DJ Haris – were the best all summer. 2007 promises four more. The hotel was built in 1985, a prestigious conference centre with all the leisure trappings, and bombed by air and sea in October 1991. Its setting, overlooking Sv Jakov and Lokrum, with the Old Town in the distance, is still as spectacular. Check the web for details.

Lazareti

Lazareti complex, Banje beach, Frana Supila 8 (020 324 633/www.lazareti.du-hr.net). **Open** *according to programme.* No credit cards. **Map** p83 B2 ❸

The best year-round nightspot in town by far is set in this old stone building, once the Lazareti quarantine barracks. Pay your 50kn at the gate – more for the major parties staged a couple of times in summer and at New Year – and head down the steps to an open courtyard under the stars. The main building is at the bottom to the right, comprising a large stage for DJ decks and live bands, a major dance area and a sturdy balcony with a bar. Drinks are standard prices. Despite the constant movement of partied-up young locals,

the building is respected – a beautiful Austro-Hungarian relief map of the coastline dated 1810 stands intact and mounted by the door. Sadly, the website is not as scrupulously maintained – see www.clubpages.net for weekly information and the Lazareti site for big events. See box p89.

Revelin Club

Revelin Fort, Sv Dominika (020 322 164/www.revelinclub.com). **Open** 9pm-2am Wed, Thur; 9pm-3am Fri, Sat. No credit cards. **Map** p83 A2 ❹

Popular with the younger crowd, the Revelin is one of the key nightspots in town. The setting couldn't be better: a 16th-century fort where the Ragusa senate convened. Outside, a terrace overlooking the twinkling lights of the old harbour is equipped with a cocktail bar in summer. Inside is jammo. A narrow corridor with a cloakroom leads to a contained dancefloor room, which you have to cross to get to the bar. If you're lucky you'll find a table in the seating area by the bar. If not, it's standing room only, so get friendly. The DJ at the back of the dance room spins winning tunes for an undiscerning, dance-hungry crowd. Things can run late – you might just stagger out and see the sun rise over the Old Town.

Arts & leisure

Art Workshop Lazareti

Lazareti complex, Banje beach, Frana Supila 8 (020 423 497/020 421 114/ www.edd.hr/en/arl.html). **Open** *varies.* **Map** p83 B2 ❶

The future of the art projects set up at the Lazareti complex is uncertain. Already both the renowned Otok Gallery and the Karentena fringe festival it staged in 2006 are said to be under threat. The main non-profit making Art Workshop, set up 20 years ago, continues to help young local creatives, organise artist-in-residence programmes and stage events, such as the iSummit in June 2007. For the short-term, its funding is assured – perhaps its future needs a little direction.

Pile & Boninovo

The area of **Pile** begins at the gate of the same name, in front the bus-choked traffic hub and taxi station of **Brsalje**, guarded by stern **Fort Lovrijenac**. Trams once clattered around here before heading up to Gruž. These days a handful of key nightspots have set up, beyond the early-closing regulations of the Old Town: **Capitano**, **Latino Club Fuego** and, further along, **Orlando Klub**. The straight main road leading west out of the Old Town, **Dr Ante Starčevića**, runs steeply parallel to the jagged rocky coast below, passing the landmark **Hilton Hotel**, opposite **Gradac Park** and the International University Centre.

Heading on towards Gruž and Lapad, the road passes the sheer drop of **Dančé Bay** balustraded on one side, and a mish-mash of

dilapidated villas and cemeteries on the other, the district known as **Boninovo**. A hundred years ago, this was a place of relaxation and a hub of academia. Above rise the steep residential streets of Middle and Upper Kono and, much higher up, Napoleon's **Imperial Fort** atop **Mount Srdj**. Before the 1991 war there was a cable car station here as well – now it's a ruin, its renovation an expensive venture and logistical nightmare. Ordnance still dots these hillsides.

Squeezed in between the hills and the approaching rugged promontory of Lapad, the main roads narrow into a major junction, traffic dividing off for the ferry terminal and bus station of Gruž, the main road north out of Dubrovnik across the Franjo Tudjman bridge, and Lapad.

Pile Gate p95

Sights & museums

Church of St Andrew

Miha Klaića 8 (020 426 029).
Map p93 D2 ❶

Facing Gradac Park, this small parish church was erected around the time that Dubrovnik was being built, from the 9th century onwards. It was later altered in the 16th century and again in the 19th, when a new entrance and rose window were added. The main attraction for visiting it today is to see Pier Giovanni's triptych *Madonna with the Saints.*

Church of St George

Zagrebačka (no phone). **Map** p93 C2 ❷

Set on the main road skirting the Old Town, this little-known church is a mixture of styles, the original one Romanesque. It contained Baroque elements too, but the altars were lost to modernisation in the 20th century. Still of sightseeing value are the two images of the Madonna dating from the 15th and 16th centuries.

Church of St Peter

Izmedju tri crkve (no phone).
Map p93 C3 ❸

This somewhat stark modern church overlooking Danče Bay was part of the Boninovo cluster of a trio of churches and two graveyards either side of Izmedju tri crkve – 'Between Three Churches'. Designed by Ivan Prtenjak in the late 19th century, its place in local lore links it to the occult rituals that took place around here at the time.

Gradac Park

Map p93 D3 ❹

Formal gardens are pretty few and far between in Dubrovnik so this sadly underused park is the nicest bit of greenery nearest the Old Town. Although somewhat rundown, its statues chipped away and its flowerbeds bare, Gradac would have bristled with Habsburg pride when it was laid out by the Austrians in the 19th century. Today it's still a casual place for quiet reflection, set back from the traffic roar of city buses chugging up and down the busy incline of Dr Ante Starčevića. In the same grounds stands the International University Centre, set up in the dark days of the Cold War, its peaceful mission of mutual understanding at one with its surroundings.

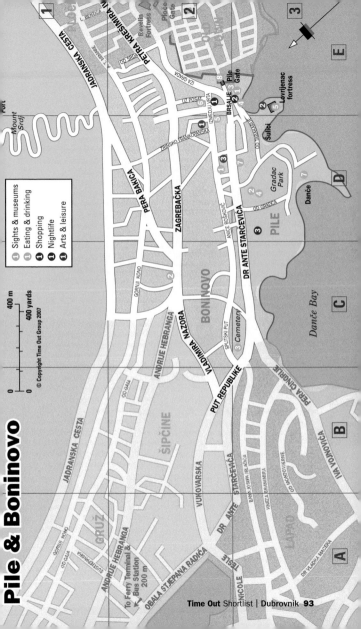

Pile & Boninovo

@ Copyright Time Out Group 2007

0   400 m
0   400 yards

- ① Sights & museums
- ① Eating & drinking
- ① Shopping
- ① Nightlife
- ① Arts & leisure

Lovrijenac Fortress

Map p93 E3 ⑤

Standing out on its own on a spit of land between the bays of Pile and Kolorina, protecting the Old Town from the west, the fort of Lovrijenac bears the proud motto *'Non bene pro toto libertas venditur auro'* – 'Liberty is not for sale, not even for gold'. To this end, a fort was built here on the site of a look-out post in the 14th century. It was reinforced by the great Old Town architect Juraj Dalmatinac a century later, after the fall of Constantinople. Soldiers stood guard round the clock. After the fall of Ragusa in the early 19th century, most of the cannons were removed by the French and Austrians and melted down. A couple are in the Museum of Military History in Vienna. Lovrijenac became a prison, a hotel, and a prison again under the Italians in World War II. After the war it was renovated and now provides a stage for the Dubrovnik Festival, in particular for open-air performances of *Hamlet*. It is otherwise closed to the public.

Mount Srdj

Map p93 D1 ⑥

Site of the illuminated cross seen high over the Old Town, Mount Srdj offers a great view to all who scale its footpath. Napoleon's Imperial Fort still stands here – but not the cable car. See box p97.

Our Lady of Dance

Dance (no phone). **Map** p93 D3 ⑦

Also known as the Church of St Mary, this is the most interesting of the churches in the locality. Here are both a nunnery and the remains of the first quarantine barracks established in Dubrovnik, when the plague was at its height. Nuns still ring the church bell to greet passing ships. Inside the church is the real treasure, a triptych by Nikola Božidarević, painted in 1517, the last work by the greatest painter of the Dubrovnik School. The image of the Virgin Mary flanked by two saints contains a self-portrait in the blade of one of the saint's swords.

Beaches

Pile is not known for its beaches. It was an industrial neighbourhood, the site of Dubrovnik's first harbour. Tanners, weavers and dyers worked in factories and warehouses outside the Old Town. Trams ferried workers up from Gruž and down the main road to the Pile Gate.

There is little evidence of this today. If anything, the little beach here is one of Dubrovnik's cleanest. **Šulići**, also known as **Penatur**, is accessed a short walk from the Pile Gate, along atmospheric, winding Od Tabakarije. This short stretch of pebble is wonderfully isolated, flanked on either side by the Lovrijenac fortress and Gradac Park, the shore lapped by greenish, clear waters. Rocks tower above. Occasionally, entertainment is provided by the local water-polo team practising for summer's Divlja Liga ('Wild League') contest between rival beaches.

The second beach here is on the other side of the Danče promontory, park and university. It's accessed along Od Graca, near the complex containing the votive church Our Lady of Danče and its art treasures from the Dubrovnik School of the 16th century, and the adjacent remains of Dubrovnik's first quarantine barracks. Nuns still ring the church bell to signal at passing ships. Just below, the rocky beach of **Danče** stretches to an open, clear sea. The bay here isn't so sheltered, so waves can be rough. Take care if you're here with children.

Atlas Club Nautika

Pile Gate

Map p93 E2 ⑧

The main entrance to the Old Town is suitably imposing, outer and inner gates intersected by a drawbridge that once was hauled up every night. The gate occupies the site of the old fortress of the same name, which stood here until the Habsburgs demolished it in 1818. The outer gate was originally an archway in the fortress wall in the early 16th century; the inner gate and bridge, built by Paškoje Miličević, pre-date it. Pile was the gate on which General Lauriston politely knocked in 1806. Its opening signalled the end of the Ragusa republic. Statues of St Blaise grace each gate; the outer one displays a trio of mysterious stone heads underneath it, two women's and one man's. The inner statue is the work of Ivan Meštrović, Croatia's most renowned sculptor of the modern era.

Eating & drinking

Atlas Club Nautika

Brsalje 3 (020 442 526). **Open** *Mid Jan-mid Dec* noon-midnight daily. **Restaurant. Map** p93 E3 ①

Just outside the Pile Gate, this is the snazziest place in town, with two panoramic terraces, impeccably staffed with starched white-tablecloth formality and, naturally, vastly expensive. For your one holiday blow-out (400kn-500kn à la carte, with wine), try and book a sea-view table: nos.30-38 on the Penatur terrace or nos.56, 57 or 64 on Lovrijenac/Brsalje. The interior dining rooms are quite plain. Chef Nikola Ivanišević insists on the freshest fish (ask for recommendations), also used in the 500kn-700kn five-course menus. Shellfish are a speciality, particularly in dishes from the Elafiti islands such as Lopud *brodet* with polenta. Cream of scampi soup with black truffles is another favourite. Desserts include strawberries in maraschino with mint or strudel with dry figs and sour cherries. Budget diners can opt for a light lunch, an Adriatic salad or pasta with mushrooms and truffles.

La Bohème

Dr Ante Starčevića 29 (020 312 688). **Open** *Mid Apr-late Sept* 11.30am-midnight daily. Closed late Sept-mid Apr. **Cocktail bar.** No credit cards. **Map** p93 D3 ②

Although since surpassed by better cocktail bars here, La Bohème can offer the unique surroundings of a stately 19th-century villa set in the formal gravel and greenery of Gradac Park. The Dubrovnik Symphony Orchestra use upstairs as a rehearsal space. The divans and armchairs of the lounge bar fill the ground-floor space. Few surprises on the drinks menu, all standard mixes at standard prices. La Bohème is crying out for someone to transform it into something really special.

Kavana Dubravka
Brsalje (020 426 319). **Open** *Summer* 10am-midnight daily. *Winter* 10am-8.30pm. **Café**. No credit cards. **Map** p93 E3 ❸

Right by the Pile Gate, with arguably the best terrace in town, the Dubravka is a local landmark. Its interior is now a modernised, sunken room brightened by shelves of colourful, sticky cakes and old photographs of the trams that used to terminate here – before the war it accommodated intellectuals, writers

and the local chess society. A spot on the sea-facing terrace is perfect for a glass of Laško and ham-and-cheese sandwich (18kn). The sweet snacks are noteworthy: a *savijača* (7kn) of apple or cherry, a slice of cake (12kn) or strawberries and cream (25kn).

Orhan
Od Tabakarije 1 (020 414 183). **Open** 11am-midnight daily. **Restaurant**. **Map** p93 E3 ❹

Another candidate for best terrace in town, the unsung Orhan can give most places a run for their money. Perched between the fortresses of Bokar and Lovrijenac, with sea waves crashing against the boulders below its summer terrace, Orhan could not be more dramatically located. Inside is neat, spacious and two-storeyed. From a lengthy menu, chef Ivića Miloš might pick out his fillet steak in gorgonzola sauce (110kn) or châteaubriand for two (240kn). There's a buffet salad bar too, with grilled peppers and aubergines. Grgić (400kn) heads a decent wine list.

Latino Club Fuego p99

Porat

*Hilton Imperial, Marijana Blažica 2
(020 320 320/www.hilton.com).* **Open**
7am-11pm daily. **Restaurant**. **Map**
p93 D2 ❺

The Hilton's stellar restaurant offers
contemporary, inventive cuisine. As
well as local treats – air-dried, smoked
ham – the accent is on the pan-seared
and the rosemary-tinted. The grilled
lamb ribs, one of several meaty delica-
cies from the lava-stone grill, have a
rosemary lard crust, the pan-seared
tuna is marinated in lime and rosemary. With an appetiser (octopus
carpaccio, grilled peppers and spicy
wild rocket, 90kn) and a main (pork
belly with vegetable caponata, 140kn)
you won't get much change from
400kn, but it's all international quality.
Also equipped with a summer terrace.

Posat

Uz Posat 1 (020 421 194). **Open**
10am-3pm, 5.30pm-midnight daily.
Restaurant. No credit cards. **Map**
p93 E2 ❻

Anywhere else, this standard local
konoba would hardly be worthy of
note, but with its setting in a spacious
garden terrace overlooking Minčeta
fortress and the City Walls, the Posat
is a handy and reasonably priced destination to know. Grilled meats are the
order of the day, mainly lamb and
chicken, prepared and garnished in the
standard, simple way.

Tovjerna Sesame

*Dante Alighieria (020 412 910/091
500 8647 mobile/www.sesame.hr).*
Open 8am-midnight daily. **Café-
restaurant**. **Map** p93 D3 ❼

A choice spot for mid-priced meals,
morning coffees and evening drinks.
Set in greenery facing the post office,
this 200-year-old building contains
tables in its front porch, its main bar
and its back restaurant. You can also
take a Buongiorno Ragusa breakfast at
an outside table. The narrow bar, its
little counter propped up by foreign
professors from the nearby university,
is decked out with charming images of

Unfinished business

In September 2006, planning
permission was given for the
renovation of the cable car on
Mount Srdj, above Dubrovnik –
15 years after the 400-metre
peak was bravely defended by
locals. The cable car had been
a popular tourist attraction.

The hillsides are dotted with
ordnance from the conflict – do
NOT wander from the footpath –
and only specialised companies
can take the job. Its expensive
completion may take years.

Dubrovnik was built at the
foothills of Mount Srdj. This
limestone crag was a barrier
between Ragusa and the rest of
the world. On it stood a fortress,
three look-out posts and, in the
1470s, a Turkish customs gate.
The symbolic little church of St
Sergius stood nearby.

Napoleon razed it in 1812. To
mark his victory over Russians
and Montenegrins here, and to
outshine the Old Town, he built
a fort. Cannons boomed out
news of his march into Moscow.

The fort became a tourist
attraction for cable-car arrivals,
and a discotheque. A large
cross, lit up at night, marks
where Croats kept Serb forces
at bay in 1991. The ragged flag
they fought for stands in the
Memorial Room of the Dubrovnik
Defenders at the Sponza Palace.

To scale Srdj, leave from
the Pile Gate onto Zrinsko
Frankopanska, over Jadranska
cesta and up the footpath. The
climb takes two hours, mainly
unshaded. Take plenty of water.

Paddling to Koločep

Sea kayaking is Dubrovnik's latest outdoor craze.

'When I arrived here tourism was reverting back to its Yugoslav mass model,' says Tamsen Resor, explaining why she set up outdoor adventure firm **Adriatic Kayak Tours** (p99) in 2005. 'There was little for the active, independent visitor. Eco-tourism didn't really exist. Experiencing the coast and islands by sea kayak seemed like a natural fit.' American Tamsen had been exploring the coves, caves and coast since 2002, the same features she and her seven-strong experienced international team now take small groups to.

Sea kayaking is Dubrovnik's major outdoor activity for tourists. Some six companies here offer tours, usually on a half-day basis with lunch thrown in. Diving requires planning and logistical know-how – a course, a certificate and heavy, potentially life-saving equipment. For sea kayaking beginners only need turn up, go through a few paddling techniques in shallow, protected waters, and it's Lokrum island for lunch.

Sea kayaks have been adapted for their use. They're more comfortable than conventional kayaks. Their length, with extra cargo capacity, allows for the kayak to move smoother and easier in a straight line. They generally accommodate a pair of paddlers. You can circumnavigate Ireland or Australia in one.

The calm waters from the Pile Gate to the verdant, car-free island of Lokrum is, under guidance, a doddle. AKT also offer sunset paddles, with wine and cheese thrown in. Children aged eight to 16 are welcome but must be accompanied by an adult.

AKT run full-day and customised group tours too – and, despite the name, not just sea kayaking. You can go white-water rafting in Montenegro's Tara River Canyon, mountain biking in Konavle and Istria, enjoy three days of kayaking and snorkelling around the Elafiti islands, and, for 2008, even try winter sea kayaking in the Bay of Kotor, Montenegro.

forgotten festivals, trams, water-polo matches and Bette Davis. The date of 1880 in the wrought iron echoes the family tradition. A cosy restaurant lined with retro holiday posters offers oyster soup (35kn), Šipan salad (60kn) and a house risotto (60kn) of clams and squid. Superb local wines.

Nightlife

Capitano

Izmedju vrta 2 (no phone). **Open** 6pm-4am Wed-Sat. No credit cards. **Map** p93 E2 **❶**

Everyone's favourite pick-up joint, this disco-bar near the Pile Gate has two more bar counters set up outside on the busy stretch of terrace. Inside it's intimate, but with plenty of room for dancing and opportunity for eye contact. Capitano made its name as the Polo, and still attracts a young, party crowd, much of it local. Commercial dance tunes feature with occasional live acts.

Latino Club Fuego

Brsalje 11 (020 312 871/091 572 9645 mobile). **Open** *Summer* 10pm-4am. *Winter* 10pm-4am Thur-Sat. No credit cards. **Map** p93 E3 **❷**

The last chance club is an all-too-easy slide down from the Capitano, by the Pile Gate. Set up in 2001, the Latino Club Fuego is well established as an after-hours destination, a popular spot for a dance, a drink and a stab at dalliance. There's nothing Latino at all about the two-floor interior, nor about the music, unless you're there for one of the carnival nights. Commercial dance music rules. The modest admission charge counts towards a drink.

Orlando Klub

Branitelja Dubrovnika 41 (020 312 674/www.klub-orlando.com). **Open** 5pm-late daily. Concert times vary. No credit cards. **Map** p93 D3 **❸**

If you thought Dubrovnik couldn't do grunge, think again. This is alternative with a capital A. The pierced and the tattooed bowl down Dr Ante Starčevića from the Pile Gate until they reach a guard hut outside an old hospital complex. Down the path, up some steps and across a garden strewn with beer cans, they find like-minded souls hanging around outside a bemuralled building emblazoned with the words: 'Fluid Between Mind & Soul'. The squat-like interior contains a stage, DJ decks and proper bar counter, with a couple of side rooms full of recalcitrant teenagers up way past their bedtime. The well managed Croatian-language website has details of upcoming gigs and DJs.

Arts & leisure

Adriatic Kayak Tours

Zrinsko-Frankopanska 6 (020 312 770/ www.adriatickayaktours.com). **Open** *Summer* varies. No credit cards. **Map** p93 D2 **❶**

A range of outdoor activities, including sea kayaking for beginners from Banje beach. See box p98.

Adventure Dalmatia

091 526 3813 mobile/091 546 4110 mobile/www.adventuredalmatia.com. **Open** *Summer* from 11am Mon; from 9am Tue, Thur, Sat; from 4pm Wed, Fri. No credit cards. **Map** p93 E3 **❷**

Sea-kayaking for beginners, given brief instruction from an experienced guide before taking off for half-a-day's adventure around the calm waters of Lokrum island. Lunch is included. Groups depart near the Lovrijenac fortress. Adventure Dalmatia also lays on longer tours, night kayaking and snorkelling. Its main office is in Split – book on the website or call the mobile.

Slavica cinema

Dr Ante Starčevića 42 (020 321 425/ www.kinematografi.org). **Open** *Summer* from 2008. No credit cards. **Map** p93 D2 **❸**

This classic open-air cinema has an equally classic bar adjoining it, both enjoying a fabulous panoramic view of Danče Bay. After the summer season of 2006, the Slavica closed for renovation during the winter. It may open in 2007 – but more likely it won't be until 2008. The bar is a godsend, whatever film happens to be playing.

DUBROVNIK BY AREA

Gruž

DUBROVNIK BY AREA

Today a transport hub, its narrow harbour road thick with traffic heading to or away from the **ferry terminal** and the **bus station**, Gruž has a history of its own.

This was a pleasant spot close to the Old Town where a Ragusan nobleman could build his villa. Orange and lemon trees lined the pathway to the Pile Gate. By the 1600s, Gruž was the great shipyard of the Ragusa republic, so vital the senate toyed with the idea of moving city business here, away from an Old Town destroyed after the earthquake of 1667.

Montenegrin raids on the villas and palaces around the nearby **Riječka Dubrovačka**, Napoleon's takeover of Ragusa, and the fall of the old order, saw Gruž decline. It was still significant enough to warrant a tram link with the Pile Gate in the early 20th century – there was once a train station here too. The rise of tourism saw Gruž harbour expand and develop. It was an obvious target for Serbs during the 1991 bombardment.

Its reconstruction and the return of tourists in significant numbers have coincided with ambitious plans for the locality. Talk centres on Riječka Dubrovačka, the narrow channel dwarfed by the new **Franjo Tudjman bridge**. The modest marina at Komolac on the south side is to be augmented by a bigger complex – if all goes to plan. There is also rumour of rebuilding the tramline, installing a car park, constructing a business centre, well out of sight of the Old Town. In the meantime, local life still revolves around the **market** opposite the ferry terminal.

Sights & museums

Church of the Holy Cross

Gruška obala 2 (020 418 118).
Map p103 C2 ①
Part of the Dominican monastery established here in the 1400s, this landmark church suffered significant damage during World War II and was renovated in the 1950s. It stands on the main road, diagonally opposite the ferry terminal.

Church of St Nicholas of the Shipyard

Gruška obala. **Map** p103 B2 ②
The great *škver*, shipyard, was established in Gruž in 1525. Each launch coincided with a service at this church, built in the early 1700s. Ships still fill the interior, in painting or model form, gold and silver, placed there by sailors in gratitude for safe passage.

Franjo Tudjman bridge

Map p103 A1 ③
The most impressive and prestigious construction in the southern Dalmatia of late, this 500-metre long, 50-metre high single-span bridge links Dubrovnik with the outside world. Bus passengers heading north pass over it, as the dramatic visual spread unfolds of the Elafiti islands on one side and Riječka Dubrovačka channel on the other. Initiated in 1990, the bridge had its first stone laid by war statesman Franjo Tudjman shortly before his death that year.

Eating & drinking

Amfora

Obala Stjepana Radića 26 (020 419 419/020 418 903). **Open** 1-10.30pm daily. **Restaurant**. **Map** p103 C2 ①
Catching the morning sun on the main harbour road, the Korda family's Amfora offers the domestic grilled treats of fish and meat, at much lower prices than you would find in the Old Town. Locals dive in at lunchtimes for their budget *marenda*, a two- (or even three-) course daily special.

Gruž market

In the same location as set after the war, a section of the ruined garden of the Gundulić summer villa, **Gruž market** (p105) is larger and cheaper than the one in the Old Town. Shoppers and occasional restaurateurs arrive here, near the ferry terminal, from early in the morning, hoping to find the best goods. Few words are exchanged with the vendors, who have come down from the Neretva delta, Konavle or Herzegovina over the border.

With all the recent social upheaval, family meals are sacrosanct, still something wholesome and stable. You'll find better cuisine at home than in many restaurants. Here is where the unpaid cooks come for ingredients.

With a little luck, locals find the best cabbage for *zelena menestra* (cabbage, smoked pork and potato), goats' cheese for salads, the best eggs for *rožata* (the local version of crème caramel) and, for traditional Ragusan orange cake, oranges from Lopud. Prices are mostly fixed and haggling doesn't tend to happen. A little discount might be easiest at the end of the working day, when vendors are looking to offload all their stock.

If you are fond of fine fish, get here by 7am, when women arrive from the Elafiti islands. The stock varies from day to day, but Fridays is usually the best. Although everyone here moans about the cost of living these days, the most expensive fish, starting from 100kn a kilo, quickly vanishes.

DUBROVNIK BY AREA

Ferata

Obala Pape Ivana Pavla II (no phone).
Open 7am-9pm Mon-Sat; 9.30am-
noon Sun. **Bar**. No credit cards.
Map p103 C2 ❷

Opposite the bus terminal, Ferata once
served the train station that stood here
– pictures of old locomotives line the
modest bar interior. In the morning
sun, it's the ideal spot for a beer before
or after a trek through Dalmatia. The
scattering of tables soon fill with backpackers and garage hands from the
nearby workshops. Not much by way
of snacks – head towards the cluster of
restaurants nearby at the market.

Glorijet

*Obala Stjepana Radića 16 (020 419
788/098 285 180 mobile).* **Open**
11.30am-10.30pm daily. No credit cards.
Restaurant. **Map** p103 C2 ❸

No hidden agenda here – just solid,
domestic cuisine at knockdown prices,
one of many choices greeting weary
bus or boat passengers if they cross the
main harbour road instead of heading
off right away to the Old Town. There
is usually a daily special, along with
the standard grilled meats and squid,
all accompanied by wine so cheap they
just have to order another.

Konoba Tobak

Vukovarska 34 (020 357 242). **Open**
7am-8pm Mon-Fri; 7am-4pm Sat.
Restaurant. **Map** p103 D3 ❹

Don't be put off by the location behind
a car wash – it's signposted from the
main road near the nos.1A, 1B or 8 bus
stops at the swimming pool – Tobak is
a little gem. Busy with local workers
brunching on the weekday 30-kn
marenda, Tobak appeals on quieter
Saturdays when visitors can choose
their table and one of half-a-dozen
equally cheap meat and fish dishes.
The accompanying glass of house
white and slices of seeded dark bread
tip the price over 60kn.

Konoba Zrinski

*Hotel Gruž, obala Stjepana Radića 33
(020 418 977).* **Open** 8am-midnight
daily. **Restaurant**. **Map** p103 C2 ❺

Near the market, a neat, modern bar
and similarly neat, modern, spacious
restaurant behind offer cheap dishes of
the seafood spaghetti (40kn) variety.
Zrinski platters (100kn), either meat or
fish, sag beneath the weight of simply
prepared offerings. You can also opt
for that day's catch at 290kn a kilo, or
ask the kitchen to prepare scampi,
shrimps or squid in the way you like.
If it's just a snack you're after, then opt
for an octopus salad (50kn) or a pan-
cake (20kn). House wine comes at 60kn
a litre, Zlatan Plavac at 150kn and
draught Karlovačko at 30kn a litre.

Mališ

Padre Perice 1 (no phone). **Open** 7am-
11pm daily. **Bar**. No credit cards.
Map p103 C2 ❻

A few steps from Gruž market and the
harbour, Mališ is the domain of traders,
early risers, revenant alcoholics and
bewildered new foreign arrivals. Prices
are fixed to suit market demands: a
draught beer (7kn) is thus cheaper than
a cappuccino (8kn). You will find it
open at 7am, you may find it in full
swing much earlier, awash with a spill
of diverse personalities still looking for
fun. It serves that one last drink or a
first coffee after a long, long night.

Porat

*Obala Stjepana Radića 30 (020 422
918/020 418 904).* **Open** Mar-Oct
7am-10pm daily. Closed Nov-Feb.
Restaurant. **Map** p103 C2 ❼

This is old-style dining, with pictures
over the bar of each dish, a sturdy hall
you could imagine filled with package
tourists c1973. Recipes and staff uni-
forms date from a similar era, although
that's not rare in Dubrovnik. The front
terrace is pleasant, though, offering a
view onto Gruž market and the
seafront, and prices differ compara-
tively little from 30 years ago. Not to
be confused with the upscale Porat, the
signature restaurant at the Hilton.

Taverna Nostromo

*Hotel Petka, obala Stjepana Radića 38
(020 410 524).* **Open** 11am-midnight
daily. **Restaurant**. **Map** p103 D2 ❽

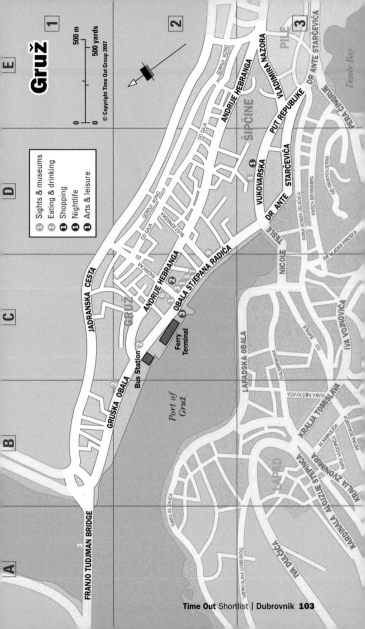

Gruž

© Copyright Time Out Group 2007

500 m
500 yards

- ● Sights & museums
- ● Eating & drinking
- ● Shopping
- ● Nightlife
- ● Arts & leisure

FRANJO TUĐMAN BRIDGE

JADRANSKA CESTA

GRUŠKA OBALA

Bus Station

Ferry Terminal

Port of Gruž

GRUŽ

ANDRIJE HEBRANGA

OBALA STJEPANA RADIĆA

OD GAJA

GORNJI KONO

SUSTJEPANSKA

RADNIČKA

ANDRIJE HEBRANGA

ŠIPČINE

PUT REPUBLIKE

VLADIMIRA NAZORA

VUKOVARSKA

DR ANTE STARČEVIĆA

DR ANTE STARČEVIĆA

TESLE

NICOLE

LAPADSKA OBALA

DALMATINSKA

IVANA MEŠTROVIĆA

IVA VOJNOVIĆA

KRALJA TOMISLAVA

KRALJA ZVONIMIRA

KARDINALA ALOJZIJA STEPINCA

IVA DULČIĆA

LAPAD

PILE

Danče Bay

FERA CINGRIJE

OD MONTOVJERNE

BANA JOSIPA JELAČIĆA

KNEZA BRANIMIRA

OD VLAHA BUKOVCA

MARIJE PL. JAGIĆ

VETRANOVIĆA

MARA PLAĆA

VETROSLAVA LISINSKOG

MARA VODOPIĆA

PERA BUDMANIJA

Sailing from Dubrovnik

Whether a new marina will be built here or not, Dubrovnik is still a prime destination for sailors. The current one (www.aci-club.hr) at Komolac, on the south side of the Riječka Dubrovačka channel, is near Gruž and the ferry terminal. It's year-round, with a pool, tennis courts, a supermarket, a store for sailing gear and showers. The Old Town is 15 minutes away by bus.

Attractive ports of call line the coast and nearby islands. For the beginner, navigation is easier here, the waters less crowded. For experts, the sailing conditions around Pelješac are ideal. Adria Coral (www.adriacoral.com), Adriatic Yacht (www.ayc.hr), Ecker (www.eckeryachting.com), Sunsail (www.sunsail.com) and Waypoint (www.waypoint-int.com) are some of the many charter companies based here. Some offer one-way charters for you to explore further without having to double back.

The other main marina (www.aci-club.hr) is on Korčula's north-east coast, near the town, and busy in

high season. You'll find easy moorings at Cavtat, by Dubrovnik airport. Lined with luxury yachts, it's near the coast of Montenegro.

The north-west coast of Lopud, one of the nearby Elafiti islands, offers anchorage and sandy beaches. Polače, in a spacious and safe bay on the west tip of Mljet, has easy moorings and a choice of restaurants. Where you moor is where you dine. It's also close to Mljet National Park.

Zaklopatica on the north coast of remote Lastovo island has easy, free moorings offered by the only restaurant, provided you eat there. On the west coast, Luka Veli Lago and Luka Malo Lago are two bays straddling a tiny road bridge connecting the islet of Prežba. There are good moorings and facilities – expect to pay 175kn a day for a ten-metre boat. A diving base and generally a welcoming drink are given by the Pension Ladesto (www.lastovo-paradise.com), which supplies the moorings and showers.

The Hotel Petka opens its restaurant to the public, a two-storey affair with a relaxed eaterie at street level and more formal dining room upstairs. Service is good in both. The downstairs taverna, with a buffet salad bar, offers quality versions of Croatian classics, with all the usual garnishes. Domestic wines at reasonable prices complete the picture.

Shopping

Bio & Bio

Mercante Centar, Vukovarska 24 (020 311 614/www.biovega.hr). **Open** 8am-8pm Mon-Fri; 8am-3pm Sat. **Map** p103 D3 **①**

The main store in town for organic, vegan, vegetarian and macrobiotic products is located on the first floor of Mercante shopping centre, near the local bus station in Šipčine, between Gruž and Pile. For soya or rice milk, miso soup or other healthy treats, this is the place. Freshly baked non-dairy croissants and cakes complement a great selection of breads. There is also a range of organic cosmetics.

Gruž market

Obala Stjepana Radića (no phone). **Open** 6am-6pm Mon-Sat; 6-11am Sun. *Fish market* 6am-noon Mon-Sat. No credit cards. **Map** p103 C2 **②**

The main market in Dubrovnik for fruit, vegetables and, alongside, fish. See box p101.

Konzum

Obala Pape Ivana Pavla II (020 433 333/www.konzum.hr). **Open** 8am-11pm Mon-Sat; 8am-1pm Sun. Closed public hols. **Map** p103 C2 **③**

One of Konzum's new superstores stands beside a car park near the ferry terminal and the bus station. Super Konzum offers pretty much everything, electrical goods as well as foodstuffs, with a bakery, butcher's, deli counter, and rows and rows of quality Croatian wine at knockdown prices. If you need to do a major shop for the week or knock together a budget barbecue, this is the place to do it. It's a short stagger to the bus stop for the Old Town – you'll need to change at the next junction for Lapad.

Franjo Tudjman bridge p101

Lapad

Lapad is Dubrovnik's playground. This verdant headland poking out into the sea offers tranquillity and outstanding views of the rocky Grebeni islets just offshore, the Elafiti islands and, on a clear day, Mljet. It is no surprise that it was here that notable Ragusan nobles built their villas. The 16th-century **summer residence of Petar Sorkočević**, overlooking Gruž, is a classic example.

Lapad's picture-perfect location was not lost on local planners four hundred years later, when the then Yugoslavia geared itself for mass tourism. Prominent resort hotels were built around Lapad's convoluted coastline. Some were of the package variety, others were more prestigious. The **Hotel Dubrovnik Palace** was a work of art even when it was built in 1972.

The conflict of the early 1990s not only saw many of these places damaged, it decimated the tourist industry. In the last five years, major companies such as Adriatic Luxury Hotels have sunk millions of euros in reconstructing these key hotels, so that their spa, restaurant and lounge bar facilities would give any venue in the Mediterranean a run for its money. Most facilities are open to all, and not, for the quality, dear. Cocktails at the **Sunset Lounge** at the Dubrovnik Palace provide an unforgettable experience. The recently opened **Bellevue** offers similar treats.

For families on a regular budget, resort hotels such as **Kompas** and those in the **Valamar** group provide easy leisure set around Lapad's beaches. These are the best equipped in Dubrovnik in terms of

Sights & museums

Church of Our Lady of Mercy

Liechtensteinov put 14 (no phone).
Map p109 E5 ❶
Down between Gospino polje and the Adriatic, towered over by the cranes currently constructing a new five-star Libertas Hotel, stands the oldest votive shrine erected by, and for, Dubrovnik's seafaring community. First mentioned in the history books in 1279, this simple medieval church was later renovated and extended in the 1600s. It has also been complemented by a Franciscan monastery next door.

Churches of St Michael in Lapad

Dr Ante Šercera 1 (no phone).
Map p109 D4 ❷
Just off the main drag of Iva Vojnovića, on the edge of Hladnica, stand two churches a few metres and nearly a millennium apart. On one side is the newest church in Dubrovnik, opened in 1999, a stark, contemporary construction. It contrasts nicely with the original Church of St Michael in Lapad, its predecessor dating from medieval times. Known to be a Romanesque structure in the 13th century, it was renovated over the centuries in the architectural styles of the time – Renaissance, Baroque – before its present eclectic appearance. Alongside is a graveyard for Lapad notables.

Eating & drinking

Aè

Šetalište kralja Zvonimira (020 437 106). **Open** 9am-1am daily. **Bar.**
No credit cards. **Map** p108 C3 ❶
Short for the Accademia del Caffè, this open-plan bar with sunken terrace is an all-day operation, popular year round. Beside the tennis courts, Aè attracts a lively crowd with acoustic music nights. As well as coffees, 32 types of chocolate, granitas, long drinks, iced milk fruit drinks and frappés, Aè offers house wine at 8kn a glass, quality

jet ski hire, inflatables, water chutes, and so on. The public beach at Lapad is a nicer experience than the one by Ploče Gate near the Old Town. It is set at the bottom of **šetalište kralja Zvonimira**, a pedestrianised street down which you'll find rows of terrace cafés and restaurants. For other destination eateries – the Levenat is the best sited – you'll have to take a taxi or buses nos.6, 6A or 7. Bus no.4 runs down **Iva Vojnovića**, passing another stretch of bars and restaurants, and terminates at the Dubrovnik Palace.

Lapad is the southern half of the twin-headed outcrop; the northern half is **Babin Kuk**. Locals refer to the whole area west of spinal **Dr Ante Starčevića** and Gruž as Lapad. This includes the residential districts closer to Gruž, such as **Montovjerna**, **Hladnica** and **Gospino polje**, places with their own communities, shops, hospitals and social interaction.

A

B

C

1

Copacabana
beach
4

IVANA PL ZAJCA

3

BABIN KUK
1

ŠETALIŠTE NIKI I MEĐA PUČIĆA

VATROSLAVA LISINSKOG

10

IVA DULČIĆA

2

KARDINALA ALOJZIJE STEPINCA

ŠETALIŠTE NIKI I MEĐA PUČIĆA

15

7 **12**

6 22

11 **25**

KRALJA ZVONIMIRA

MATA VODOPIĆA

Lapad Bay

Lapad
beach

LAPAD

PETRA ZORANIĆ

Vis
beach

ISPOD PETKE

3

1

MASARYKOV PUT

IVANSKA

2 **2**

25
24

4

① Sights & museums
① Eating & drinking
❶ Shopping
❶ Nightlife
❶ Arts & leisure

500 m

0

0

500 yards

© Copyright Time Out Group 2007

5

Roxy p117

labels Plavac Mali (180kn) and Postup (200kn) by the bottle, standard cocktails (40kn-50kn), bottled Beck's (14kn) and Guinness (22kn), sandwiches (15kn-20kn) including domestic spicy salami, and 45kn breakfasts.

Belfast Celtic Bar

Marka Marulića 21 (no phone). **Open** 6.30am-midnight daily. **Bar.** No credit cards. **Map** p109 D3 ②

An unusual find, this, in a little row of businesses between Lapad market and the shopping centre. A proper bar for Celtic supporters, of which there are many in Catholic Croatia, it displays authentic souvenirs. On the walls are the first issue of the club's official magazine *The Celtic View*, a signed ball and shirt, a *Daily Record* from 1967, and a document inviting Josip and Ornela as members of the Motherwell branch of the Celtic Supporters' Club. Guinness (20kn) by the bottle. Signposted from the main road.

Belvedere

Iva Vojnovića 58 (020 311 761/091 572 9439 mobile). **Open** 10.30am-midnight daily. **Restaurant.** **Map** p109 D3 ③

A handy place on the main drag, well run and well priced, with the lights of Gruž harbour twinkling through the windows. Mozzarella with fried rocket (39kn), sirloin steak carpaccio (55kn) and octopus salad (50kn) feature among the appetisers. Meats are many: chicken with gorgonzola sauce (50kn); pork fillet stuffed with smoked ham and ricotta (70kn); veal medallions with asparagus and carrots (75kn). Flat mushrooms and salmon embellish the gnocchi *mare e monti* (45kn), truffle and mushroom cream flavour the ravioli (45kn). The quality, for these prices, is notable. And then there's that view...

Bistro Riva

Lapadska obala 20 (no phone). **Open** 9am-midnight daily. **Restaurant.** No credit cards. **Map** p109 E3 ④

Year-round cheapie located behind a walled-in courtyard over the water from Gruž harbour. In summer tourists

tucking into Dalmatian-style scampi (105kn) and beefsteak 'America' (with egg and fried potatoes; 90kn) fill the terrace. In winter, the action moves inside, as students fill up on the 30kn *marenda* daily lunches, choice of ten pizzas (25kn-40kn) and pastas (40kn-45kn). Usual local standards complement the Italian bias of the menu.

Blidinje

Lapadska obala 21 (020 358 794/ 099 212 6433 mobile/098 428 901 mobile). **Open** 9am-midnight daily. **Restaurant.** **Map** p109 E3 ⑤

A real find, opened in the summer of 2006. Facing Gruž harbour across the water, Blidinje comprises a rustic ground-floor space of two dozen covers, and two first-floor terraces with wonderful views of the marina and hills beyond. Carnivores should order veal, lamb or pork slow-cooked in the open oven – having given the kitchen a two-hour notice. The mixed grill for two (160kn), as good as any in town, would feed three. It's a pizzeria too, with plenty of choice. Considering the quality and location, prices are more than reasonable.

Casa Bar

Šetalište Niki i Meda Pucića 1 (020 435 353). **Open** *Mar-Oct* 9am-1am daily. Closed Nov-Feb. **Bar-restaurant.** **Map** p108 C3 ⑥

Putting your feet up on the sea wall, overlooking the moonlit waves with a beer in front of you, is one of the pleasures of the venues tucked around Lapad beach – and this is the best one. Calling itself a bar-restaurant although it serves mainly lunchtime snacks and then only in high season, the Casa is a well-known local and used as such. In fact, its closure during the winter months leaves a bit of a gap. At its best in the shoulder season, when there's a nice buzz around the bar counter.

Eden

Kardinala Alojzija Stepinca 54 (020 411 160/020 435 133). **Open** *Mar-Dec* noon-11pm daily. Closed Jan, Feb. **Restaurant.** **Map** p108 C2 ⑦

New Med cuisine

'This takes Dubrovnik to the next level,' suggests head chef Steve Pieters, sweeping his hand in a gesture that takes in the bright, imaginative, open-plan **Vapor** restaurant (p118) he now handles, the dishes of perfectly presented, immaculately conceived Med-based creations on tables perched over a wide-open Adriatic, the layers of the five-star boutique **Bellevue Hotel** above and below, and the bright blue beyond. At 35, he has every right to feel proud.

Having worked in his 17-year career at Zürich's prestigious Dolder Grand and at several establishments in the Leading Hotels of the World roster, the South African has been placed in charge of what might just become the top dining spot on the Adriatic. It's early days. The Bellevue was only opened in February 2007 and has yet to be tested over the course of a summer season. By then Steve will also have the sea-level grill restaurant Nevera to take care of, set up down below on the Bellevue's semi-private stretch of beach.

But the signs are good and the ingredients are right. 'We want to bring the concept away from set menus,' Steve continued. 'It's a case of tweaking traditional recipes. We're sourcing as much locally as possible. Tuna from Zadar, truffles from Istria, shellfish from Pelješac. We also shop right here in Dubrovnik for the freshest fish, fruit and vegetables.'

A concise daily menu may offer an appetiser of monkfish carpaccio with caviar vinaigrette on Sicilian eggplant caponata, or a lobster broth prepared Sicilian-style with cinnamon, garlic and sundried chillis. It might then move on to seared langoustine tails topped with a sauce of clams poached in chardonnay cream or a rack of lamb and crust of sundried olive oil and wild rosemary, with caramelised shallots and roasted garlic in tarragon jus. On this given day the vegetarian choice was a piccata of zucchini and forest mushrooms on Milanese risotto. Don't be afraid to test the kitchen, though, and ask for something off-menu. They like a challenge.

Design touches by Renata Štrok – a caged goldfish, a palm tree, offbeat art – avert the diner's eye from the floor-to-ceiling flood of sky and sea. The next level after this is going to be hard to imagine.

Near the upper entrance to the Kompas Hotel, the Eden is a comfortable place in which to enjoy seafood, steak and superior starter dishes, not least from its panoramic roof terrace festooned with greenery. The interior is by no means shabby either, all bright colours and modern art on the walls. Frog's legs, anchovies on toast and lobster soup feature among the starters, mains include beefsteak with lobster (120kn) and a fondu for two (180kn). Quality labels (Grgić 350kn, Zlatan Plavac Barrique 290kn) amid the local wines.

Fellini

Marka Marulića 6/Mata Vodopića (020 437 099). **Open** 11.30am-midnight daily. **Restaurant.**
Map p108 C3 ⑧
This modern restaurant surrounded by a large, sunny terrace is popular all year round. Fellini started out as a typical trattoria, checked tablecloths and all, but has since expanded to include many fish and meat specialities. The chicken breast in gorgonzola sauce stands out, as do the mushrooms stuffed with shrimp and topped with a toasted cheese melt. Most dishes won't cost you 60kn and can be accompanied by a choice of local wines. Set on Mata Vodopića, with a Marka Marulića postal address.

King Richard's Pub

Josipa Kosora (020 419 577). **Open** noon-1am daily. **Bar.** Map p109 D4 ⑨
Once a busy pub, popular with locals, is now somewhat underused, accentuated by its grand interior. A stroll from Iva Vojnovića, King Richard's stands amid modern residential housing, two floors of faux-historic detail in dark wood, also used for the long bar counter. Somehow Kilkenny is more expensive than Guinness on draught. You can also plump for Erdinger and Strongbow, wines include Pošip Čara and Zlatan Plavac, and whiskies Black Bush, Glen Grant and rare Johnnie Walker blue. Mains are meaty (rump-steak 75kn, King Richard's beef 95kn), with pastas and salads too.

Komin

Iva Dulčića 136 (020 448 613/020 435 636/098 345 777 mobile/www. restaurant-komin.com). **Open** noon-midnight daily. **Restaurant.**
Map p108 B2 ⑩
A quality, traditional local restaurant tucked away behind the big hotels on Babin Kuk, signposted from the main road. Pleasantly surrounded by greenery, a playground and local *boules* ground, Komin boasts a stone terrace and two dining areas, one a modern extension for the summer overflow. A fireplace and centrepiece grill in the main room give a rustic feel, accentuated by an offering of succulent meats traditionally prepared with hot coals, fresh fish, and plenty of shellfish as starters. Dingač, Babić and Pošip among the wines.

Konavoka

Šetalište kralja Zvonimira 38 (020 435 105/098 427 814 mobile). **Open** Mid Mar-mid Oct 11am-midnight daily. Closed Mid Oct-mid Mar. **Restaurant.**
Map p108 C3 ⑪
Popular eaterie halfway along the main drag from Lapad beach, the Konavoka comprises two terraces, one at street level overlooking the passing holiday makers, the other on the roof, decked out with house plants. All the usual favourites line the menu, grilled meats, squid, fish dishes – if you're ordering the fishermen's soup as well as a main, do bring an appetite. They go to town on the pancakes. A holiday buzz and post-beach atmosphere reign.

Konoba Atlantic

Kardinala Alojzija Stepinca 42 (020 435 726). **Open** 11.30am-midnight daily. **Restaurant. Map** p108 C2 ⑫
Near the Eden, the pleasingly modest Atlantic specialises in Italian food – and in particular a variety of imaginative sauces to accompany its pastas. Seafood, lobster, cuttlefish-ink, salmon-and-prawn, walnut-and-prawn, it's all varied and well priced. They even offer gnocchi with rabbit sauce. The seafood plate (98kn) is huge, the grilled meats likewise. Half-a-dozen tables sit on a

thin slice of terrace, while inside is cosy, wooden and nautically themed. Vrbnička Zlahtina (140kn) and Zlatan Plavac (180kn) are among the wines.

Konoba Dalmata
Šetalište kralja Zvonimira/Kralja Tomislava (no phone). **Open** *Summer* noon-midnight daily. **Restaurant**. **Map** p108 D3 ⑬
At the junction of the two main roads heading towards Lapad beach, this rather spacious neighbourhood restaurant – enclosed terrace, two floors – attracts a fair amount of trade from the hotels nearby. Grills are its speciality, in particular chops (lamb, pork) as well as beefsteak and pepper steak (60kn-120kn), with a humungous fish platter for two (299kn) to satisfy seafood fans. Pricier than the smaller places around the corner up on Kardinala Alojzija Stepinca, but worth the extra kunas for the most part.

Konoba Primorka
Nikole Tesle 8 (020 356 176). **Open** 9.30am-11pm Mon-Sat; 11am-6pm Sun. **Restaurant**. **Map** p109 E3 ⑭
Near the Minčeta department store by the Gruž harbour waterfront, the Primorka offers the best of local, home cooking at less than half the price of places you'll find in the Old Town. If there are no tables free on the garden terrace, the ones in the atmospheric vaulted rustic interior are equally pleasant. On offer are a daily 30kn *marenda* brunch, and dishes such as beef tongue in caper sauce, and pork and beans. The minced lamb in cabbage leaves, *šarma*, is also a favourite.

Levanat
Šetalište Niki i Meda Pucića (020 435 352/098 427 794 mobile). **Open** Mar-Oct 10.30am-midnight. Closed Nov-Feb. **Restaurant**. **Map** p108 B2 ⑮
Could easily take the prize for the most perfectly located restaurant in all Dubrovnik, panoramically positioned in the bay between Lapad and Babin Kuk. True, it's four flights of stone steps from the signpost on the main road – walk round the coastal path

from Lapad beach instead – but the Levanat is worth it. A few imaginative touches to Marija Sutić's menu – prawns flavoured with honey and sage, an appetiser of fried rocket and mozzarella – embellish the fabulous holiday experience of a table outside or inside a stone, candlelit interior renovated in the winter of 2006.

Mamma Mia
Bana Josipa Jelačića 37A (020 420 404/www.dubrovnik-advance.com/ mamma-mia). **Open** 9am-midnight. **Restaurant**. **Map** p109 F4 ⑯
A large selection of pizzas prepared in a wood-fire oven in simple surroundings. Grilled meats, pastas and salads are also available. Not a bad place for breakfast either, if you're staying in a private room here on the border between Lapad and Gruž – Mamma Mia does *pancerote* and sandwiches as well as providing classy coffee.

Mirakul
Iva Vojnovića 39 (no phone). **Open** 9am-1am daily. **Bar**. No credit cards. **Map** p109 D4 ⑰
One of a row of half-a-dozen smart but similar bars on the Iva Vojnovića strip popularised by local youth far away from the tourist beat. Mirakul lines up alongside Cohiba, Paradiso, Apollo, Petrunjela and XLNT. Fashionable twentysomethings fraternise with the opposite sex in spruce surroundings, with a couple of flat-screen TVs (sport, fashion) competing with a background of conversation-level domestic pop sounds for entertainment. However mainstream, it's still good to see life going on beyond the Old Town.

Orka
Lapadska obala 11 (098 243 600 mobile/www.orka-du.hr). **Open** 7.30am-4am daily. **Bar**. No credit cards. **Map** p109 E3 ⑱
A young crowd frequents this split-venue disco-bar overlooking the Gruž waterfront from the Lapad side. By day it's relaxing, the only lively discussion taking place around the MP3 machine and gossip about who was getting

Sundowners with a view

For those not used to the high-end surroundings of the Dubrovnik Palace, the **Sunset Lounge** (p118) may come as a shock, not least after the bone-shaking ride on rickety old city bus no.4 from the Pile Gate to its terminus here. Walking through the swish lobby in reasonably smart dress (T-shirts OK, shorts and flip-flops a no-no), your eyes are immediately drawn to a floor-to-ceiling panoramic glass façade of idyllic sea-blue view, interrupted by the occasional boat drifting towards one of the lush Elafiti islands. On a clear day you can see Mljet. It's not a painting and you're not dreaming.

Find a chair in the vast, chic interior and take a drinks menu. Cocktails are 48kn-56kn, Mojitos, Manhattans, Daiquiris, 35 in all. A BBC (Bailey's, banana and coconut) or a West Indian punch (white and gold Bacardi, banana liqueur, orange and pineapple juices) hit the spot in summer.

There are also unusual Croatian specialities, such as specialist brandies made by the Perković family, flavoured by carob from Komiža on Vis, figs from Šibenik or young walnuts from Dalmatia.

Wines start from a basic 15kn (Maraština Crvik, Kaštelet) to the best local labels rarely found by the glass (Dingač 35kn, Pošip Čara 32kn), beers from a Bavaria (18kn) to a Leffe (32kn). Wines and beers are offered half-price in happy hour from 3 to 5pm.

Snacks are not such a snip – 65kn for a tuna sandwich – but this is once-in-a-holiday stuff, and you may as well go the whole hog and order up a half- or full bottle of Moet et Chandon (490kn/720kn) and have done with it.

All flavours of Absolut vodkas and vintage malts line the shelves. As the sun sinks and the mood mellows, you're bound to linger until the piano player comes on in the evening.

fresh with who in the intimate back seats by the fish tank. By night the action gets a little more frenzied, particularly as the music pumps in a separate room up a flight of stone steps. Newcomers to this whale-themed establishment can look forward to a wonderful view of the harbour and Franjo Tudjman bridge beyond the expanse of window.

Orsan Yacht Club

Marina Orsan, Ivana pl Zajca 2 (020 435 933/020 411 880/098 243 717 mobile/www.orsan.cjb.net). **Open** 9.30am-midnight daily. **Restaurant**. **Map** p109 D2 ⑲

Another prime candidate for the best-located restaurant on the Lapad peninsula, Orsan is part of the yacht club of the same name on this side of Gruž Bay. A dozen tables are set on a sea-lapped terrace under the shade of a huge pine tree, a summer retreat enjoyed by cats and diners. There are places inside if it's raining. Menu highlights include oyster soup, octopus salad, lobster and Dalmatian rib-eye steak. The wines surely can't stay at 2006 prices (house red or white 50kn! Dingač 150kn!) or Orsan will go out of business. Gooey puddings (walnut or chocolate pancakes, knickerbocker glory) extend the meal past bedtime.

Pergola

Kralja Tomislava 1 (020 436 848/ 098 243 761 mobile/www.dubrovnik-advance.com/pergola). **Open** 11am-midnight daily. **Restaurant**. **Map** p109 D3 ⑳

A standard but nonetheless worthwhile restaurant near the junction with the street leading to Lapad beach. Shellfish, scampi and fresh fish by the kilo dominate a decent menu. There are grills and pastas too, with a couple of meat-free variations. The dishes are well presented and served in a pleasant interior, accompanied by a generous range of domestic wines. You won't be praising the place in postcards but you're guaranteed to be satisfyingly replete after an afternoon down on the beach.

Roxy

Bana Josipa Jelačića 11 (020 421 754). **Open** 6pm-1.30am daily. **Bar**. No credit cards. **Map** p109 F4 ㉑

The main rockers' hangout, the Roxy celebrated 20 years of hard-core drinking in 2006. Set on a small stretch of street lined with party bars (Casanova, Boogie Woogie, Ferrari) near the main junction into Lapad, the Roxy displays letters from the Beatles Fan Club, an old Animals album and an original *Penny Lane* 45, framed and mounted. There's a Seeburg jukebox, too, just for show – the aural background from the CD player is at conversation level.

Sedna Pizzeria

Hotel Kompas, šetalište kralja Zvonimira 56 (020 352 000/www.hotel-kompas.hr). **Open** 10.30am-midnight daily. **Restaurant**. **Map** p108 C3 ㉒

One of the many attractions at the nine-floor leisure complex of the seafront Hotel Kompas is this terrace pizzeria. Most customers just use it for drinks, a landmark spot for a lazy coffee overlooking the beach, but they can also order from a range of Dalmatian grilled specialities, seafood and, of course, pizzas. The Sedna does a nice line in sticky cakes and desserts too.

Spice Lounge

Hotel Bellevue, Pera Čingrije 7 (020 330 000/fax 020 330 100/www.hotel-bellevue.hr). **Open** 9am-midnight daily. **Bar-restaurant**. **Map** p109 F5 ㉓

Occupying an adjoining space with the Med fusion restaurant Vapor (p118) and enjoying a similar jaw-dropping view out to sea, the Bellevue's Spice Lounge is as fussy about its cocktails as its upscale snacks. The latter come courtesy of Steve Pieters and his team, so 'snacks' is doing it a complete disservice. Pan-seared Argentine beef carpaccio marinated in wild herbs garnished with pickled ginger is what we're talking about. As for the drinks, your choice starts at a Black Russian (50kn), Side Car (65kn) and three dozen standards on the menu – or get the barman to mix according to your mood.

Sunset Lounge

Hotel Dubrovnik Palace, Masarykov put 20 (020 430 000/www.dubrovnik palace.hr). **Open** noon-1am daily. **Bar**. **Map** p108 A4 ㉓

That fabulous sunset view, fashionable surroundings, a piano player – and happy-hour drinks in the afternoon. See box p115.

Taverna Maslina

Hotel Dubrovnik Palace, Masarykov put 20 (020 430 000/www.dubrovnik palace.hr). **Open** 11am-11pm daily. **Restaurant. Map** p108 A4 ㉕

Not the most prestigious of the dining options around this five-star hotel complex but, located down towards the sea with impeccable views and poolside seating, perhaps your first choice should you want to dine here. The design is modern Mediterranean, the fare on offer likewise, light seafood and grilled-meat treats put together with just the right sprinkle of oil and addition of greenery. Quick bites offered during the day too.

Teatar

Iva Vojnovića 72 (020 436 220). **Open** 10.30am-midnight daily. **Restaurant. Map** p109 D3 ㉖

This expansive restaurant on the main road is invariably filled with local customers of all generations, thanks to a suitably extensive menu and absolutely silly prices. Pizzas come in two sizes (25kn-35kn), the Teatar version with all the toppings; a rumpsteak is 55kn and a portion of crabs 50kn. Soups (12kn) include chickpea and lentil, while desserts feature pancakes, strudel and traditional Dalmatian *rožata*. Wines start at an equally reasonable 80kn a bottle, with all the classic domestic varieties (Ivan Dolac, Dingač, Plavac Blato) further up the scale. The friendly service is reasonably swift considering the number of tables to be waited on here.

Time Out

Iva Vojnovića 23 (no phone). **Open** 8.30am-midnight daily. **Bar**. No credit cards. **Map** p109 D4 ㉗

A handy sports bar and terrace by the no.4 bus stop on the main road. Framed football memorabilia – a Hajduk Split top, a Forza Juve scarf – decorates the walls of its rooms, the back one given over to a billiards table and table football, and a large TV screen complemented by comfy sofas. The main room, naturally, is thick with cigarette smoke from that first coffee to bedtime. An enclosed, expansive porch area allows fresh air and convivial space for post-match debate.

El Toro

Iva Vojnovića 5 (020 332 818). **Open** 9am-midnight daily. **Café-restaurant**. No credit cards. **Map** p109 D4 ㉘

Spanish-themed but also a pizzeria, El Toro makes up for this dichotomy by offering a twin-level terrace with a view, and a cosy interior in modern style. It's a nice place to spend time, whatever's on the menu. Many use El Toro as a café, musing beneath the bullfighting images. It's standard domestic drinks, mind, and little from Spain or Italy. The pizzas won't win any awards but they're cheap and filling. In July, frankly, any terrace will do.

Van

Šetalište kralja Zvonimira 40 (no phone). **Open** 9.30am-midnight daily. **Café**. No credit cards. **Map** p108 C3 ㉙

Van, as in Vincent van Gogh, the most prominent of the many cafés and restaurants lining the path down to the beach. A large terrace with swing seating, centrepieced by a public fountain contrasts with a tiny interior just big enough to accommodate a television. Van stays open in winter, offering a range of hot chocolates, but it's the rare provision of Croatia's best wines by the glass (Dingač 35kn, Babić 25kn) that merits most praise. Ice-creams, pies and cakes reward well-behaved children after a morning by the sea.

Vapor

Hotel Bellevue, Pera Čingrije 7 (020 330 000/fax 020 330 100/www.hotel-bellevue.hr). **Open** noon-3pm, 6-10pm daily. **Restaurant. Map** p109 F5 ㉚

Copacabana beach p120

Steve Pieters' kitchen team at the newly opened Bellevue provide outstanding Mediterranean cuisine with an imaginative twist – and a fabulous sea view. See box p112.

Wind

Lapadska obala 29 (no phone). **Open** 9.30am-midnight daily. **Bar**. No credit cards. **Map** p109 D2 ③

This pleasant little year-round pit stop stands where main roads meet at the Lapad edge of Gruž harbour. A young clientele gather in the traditional brick interior, sucking on cheap draught Bavaria beer and enjoying the occasional game of darts. There are bottles of Istrian Favorit too, rarely seen in these parts. Wines start from 80kn a bottle, with a couple of nicer labels also available. There is a terrace at the front, admittedly exhaust-filled, in which to enjoy a quiet glass and contemplate the Gruž waterfront.

Shopping

Lapad market

Šetalište kralja Tomislava/Mata Vodopića (no phone). **Open** 7am-2pm daily. **Map** p109 D3 ①

Lapad's sunken market square can be found where the pathway to the beach meets the main road to the Old Town, kralja Tomislava. Most mornings you will find locals picking up the usual bags of apples and tomatoes but on Sundays a handful of stalls are given over to bric-a-brac – books, postcards, stamps, medals – and you might find a more characterful souvenir here than is otherwise available on Stradun.

Lapad Shopping Centre

Kralja Tomislava 7 (020 438 088). **Open** 9am-7.30pm Mon-Fri; 10am-2pm Sat. **Map** p109 D3 ②

This multi-level modern centre stands within easy reach of Lapad beach. A handful of outlets allow those who arrived lightly luggaged to stock up on fashion essentials. There's a Benetton, several shoe shops (Croatian and Italian), as well as jewellery and accessories outlets. At chemist chain DM you'll find perfumes, cosmetics and selection of health-food products. Browse for a soundtrack to your sunbathing at CD and DVD shop Kult. Cafés have set up tables outside at street and lower-ground levels.

Best beach fun in Lapad

Copacabana beach

Lapad was built on beaches. The hotels around the edges of the headland earn their living from their access to the shore.

The best equipped beach is the **Copacabana**, a half-moon of pebbles and gravel set in Seka Bay. Facing Daksa island on the north side of Lapad, it serves the cluster of hotels in Babin Kuk, in particular the newly rebranded family resort, the **Valamar Club Dubrovnik**. Although the water here isn't as pristine as elsewhere – Seka Bay also faces the Daksa Canal, through which ferries pass en route to Gruž – the Copacabana is fun. Parachute boat rides, water chutes, canoes, jet skis, pedalos and banana rides provide high-action entertainment. **Navis Undewater Explorers** diving centre is also based here. Nearby is a signposted path down to a naturist beach, **Cava**.

The Copacabana is one of the settings for summer's Divlja Liga, the 'Wild League' of waterpolo matches between rival beaches.

The main public beach is **Lapad**. Surrounded by the **Kompas** hotel and its terrace pizzeria the **Sedna**, it's very family-friendly. Showers, sunloungers and sunshades dot the shingle surface, the shallow waters overseen by lifeguards. The pedestrianised shade of šetalište kralja Tomislava, its bouncy play area, internet park and tennis courts, are nearby. In the other direction, the rocks beside the Niki i Meda Pucića promenade allow for nude sunbathing.

Around the bay, hotels have private, pebbly beaches they part rent to the public. You can go sea kayaking from the **Adriatic** and hire jet skis from **Vis beach** near the **Splendid**. Adjacent is **Vila beach**, sandy, and ideal for a local game of picigin, a cross between keepie-uppie and volleyball.

The **Bellevue** has its own curve of shingle and sand, soon to open as a restaurant, the **Nevera**, and a private beach bar, the **Grota**. Perhaps this off-limits approach is the shape of things to come.

Nightlife

Exodus

Iva Dulčića 39 (020 448 355). **Open**
early May-late Sept 10.30pm-4.30am
Thur-Sat. Closed late Sept-early May.
No credit cards. **Map** p108 B1 **❶**

The main nightspot on Babin Kuk,
hidden amid the hotel complex, is a big,
bright, mainstream disco for young
Croats and holidaymakers. Just follow
the beam of light traced over the sky
above Copacabana beach. The DJs
won't spring any surprises amid the
barrage of house and techno, but the
prices aren't silly, the dress codes aren't
strict and there's a sea to flop into when
the sun starts to rise.

Orlandinjo Club

*Hotel Dubrovnik Palace, Masarykov
put 20 (020 430 000).* **Open** 9pm-4am
daily. **Map** p108 A4 **❷**

The fashionable nightlife element of
the upscale leisure attractions found at
the five-star Hotel Dubrovnik Palace.
The emphasis is on live music – more
often than not jazz – rather than DJ
decks, but it's all pretty mellow, satis-
fied couples extending the evening
over a couple of glasses of quality wine.
Cocktails are of similar high standard
to the ones served earlier in the day at
the Sunset Lounge (p118).

Arts & leisure

Adriatic Sea Kayaking

*020 438 666/091 329 3232 mobile/
www.adriatic-sea-kayaking.com. Day
tours from Hotel Adriatic (Masarykov
put 9).* **Open** *daily tours 15 May-
15 Oct* 8.30/9am-1pm daily. Closed
16 Oct-16 May. **Map** p109 B3 **❶**

Setting off from Lapad beach by the
Hotel Adriatic, Edi Brkić and his Adria
Adventure team take beginners on a
light and easy paddle to the verdant
nearby island of Lokrum, where lunch
is taken, and back again. Another tour
goes around the coast of the Elafiti
island of Koločep, which you reach by
speedboat. ASK also organise longer
tours of the Elafiti islands for different
kayaking levels.

Blue Planet Diving

*Hotel Dubrovnik Palace, Masarykov put
20 (091 899 973 mobile/098 991 3621
mobile/www.blueplanet-diving.com).*
Open *early May-late Oct* 9am-7pm
daily. Closed late Oct-early May. No
credit cards. **Map** p108 A4 **❷**

One of the best options for beginners
and families who wish to try their hand
at scuba diving. Blue Planet offers
Professional Association of Diving
Instructors' (PADI) certificates for all
levels, including basic ones for eight-
to 11 year olds. Experienced divers can
go on half-day, full-day or night diving
trips to the nearby reefs and coves of
Koločep and Sv Andrija, advanced
ones to the *Taranto* World War II ship-
wreck on the reef islet of Grebeni.
Moray and conger eels, groupers and
lobsters provide visual entertainment
in the 30-metre visibility of the clear
waters of the southern Adriatic.

Lapad cinema

*Eugena Kumičića (020 423 330/www.
kinematografi.org).* **Open** according
to programme. No credit cards.
Map p108 C1 **❸**

Set behind the Marina Orsan, this is
one of a handful of open-air cinemas
around Dubrovnik with seasonal programmes from June to September. Rain
stopped play is a rare but occasional
possibility – otherwise you can count
on a regular programme of subtitled
local and international releases in
charmingly old-school surroundings.

Navis Underwater Explorers

*Copacabana beach (020 356 501/098
919 7402 mobile/099 350 2773
mobile/www.navisdubrovnik.com).*
Open *May-Oct* 9am-7pm daily.
Closed Nov-Apr. No credit cards.
Map p108 B1 **❹**

One of the first private diving companies to set up in Croatia, Navis is run
by Petra Podkubovsek who oversees a
trusted staff of PADI-trained diving
instructors. Advanced divers are taken
out to war-time and Ancient Greek
wrecks. Navis is also happy to advise
on certificates and courses.

Badija p125

Trips

Cavtat

The southernmost resort in Croatia,
Cavtat is an old Greek and Roman
settlement, sacked by tribes in the
seventh century. Refugees flooded
to Ragusa and built Dubrovnik.
Today Cavtat is best known as the
birthplace of fin-de-siècle painter
Vlaho Bukovac, whose gallery on
the Riva (020 478 646, open summer
9am-1pm, 5-9pm daily, winter 9am-
1pm daily, 10kn) belonged to his
father. A bright collection of
frescoes and portraits awaits.
The other key sight is the **Račić
Mausoleum** (020 478 646, summer
10am-noon, 6-8pm Mon-Sat, 10am-
noon Sun), built by 20th-century
sculptor Ivan Meštrović for local
notables. Set on a hilltop, it's a
masterpiece in white marble
dominating the town cemetery.

Many also head here for diving
centre **Epidaurum** (020 471 386,
www.epidaurum-diving-cavtat.hr),
outside Cavtat. Roman and Greek
remains lie beneath a clear sea. The
centre offers other water sports too.
Although Cavtat is an easy day
trip from Dubrovnik – by hourly
bus No.10 (40mins, 12kn) or a
boat from the old harbour (50mins,
30kn) – you may want to stay at the
stylish six-room **Villa Kvarternik**
(Kvarternikova 3, 020 479 800,
www.dub.iz.hr).

Eating & drinking

Leut
Trumbićev put 13 (020 478 477).
Open *Feb-Dec* 10am-midnight daily.
Closed Jan. **Restaurant**.
The top spot in town offers superior
versions of Dalmatian classics plus six
set menus (110kn-260kn), the dearest

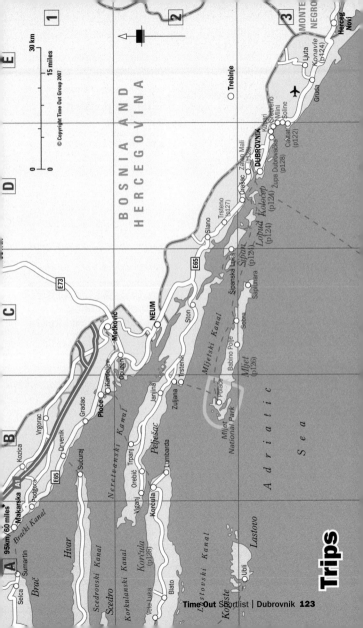

with squid and grilled lobster. Light lunches and superb cold platters (local smoked ham and cheese, octopus, mussels) reward a morning at the beach.

Elafiti islands

The easiest getaway is a boat for the three (barely) inhabited islands of the 14-isle Elafiti archipelago: **Koločep**, **Lopud** and **Šipan**.

Ferries from Gruž are geared for islanders and workers – super-cheap but infrequent. To do all three islands, head to the old harbour and find a fish picnic trip. Prices (250Kn, 180Kn without the picnic) and departure times (10am out, 6pm back) are pretty standard. Unlimited free drink for the three hours at sea is part of the package, so don't opt for a rowdy crowd if you're after peace and quiet – it's an eight-hour day and there's no escape. Given the right passengers, it's the ideal way to see the islands, and the fish is fresh and plentiful.

The first stop, Koločep, home to 150 people, offers steep cliffs, wind-carved caves and shaded walking trails for an hour. You get three hours on the sandy beaches and sea promenade of Lopud. The final hour, on Šipan, should be longer. This unspoiled island has its own dialect, spoken by locals who still live from growing melons.

Eating & drinking
Kod Marka
Šipanska luka, Šipan (020 758 007). **Open** *Summer* 11am-midnight daily. *Winter* varies. **Restaurant**. No credit cards.

Best spot on the islands, bar none. Marko Prižmić cooks fish delivered fresh by local fishermen to his terrace *konoba*. Order sea urchins a day in advance or have a look at the lobsters in the fishtank and suggest which you might like on your plate. There's a daily catch too. Marko is the perfect host – aficionados plan annual holidays around dining here on the terrace.

Konavle
Eating & drinking
Konoba Konavoski Komin
Velji Do (020 479 607/098 312 449 mobile). **Open** noon-midnight daily. **Restaurant**.

Elafiti islands

The stone-house villages of Konavle, near the airport, and Montenegrin and Bosnian borders, excel in traditional, family-run restaurants. These are not tacky – locals fill the place – and make best use of the products grown in this fertile area. Komin is one such, its back terrace overlooking uninterrupted nature. Dishes are slow-cooked in an ancient kiln-like oven, pots heated under coals before your meat (veal a speciality) octopus or vegetables is added and left for an hour or so. Phone your order ahead. Home-grown salads, domestic cheeses, bread and tomatoes round off the experience.

Korčula

A medieval fortress, centrepieced by the slim belltower of **St Mark's Cathedral**, protects the riches on Korčula. So lush with dark pine forests, vineyards and olive groves the ancient Greek settlers called it *Kerkyra Melaina* ('Black Corfu'), Korčula has managed to avoid the tourist-trap tendencies of its Greek namesake 300 miles to the south.

Korčula is a relaxing getaway, best enjoyed by an older generation of tourist. The main town of the same name, on the north-eastern tip of the island facing the Pelješac peninsula, is the most popular destination in the Dubrovnik region after Dubrovnik itself, with which it is often compared.

Unlike Dubrovnik, Korčula was governed by the Venetians, who laid out the pristine, compact Old Town. This was the supposed birthplace of Marco Polo. Whether the famed traveller was born here in 1254 isn't certain but the story has elements of truth. A museum is expected to open by 2008.

Entering from the south, you pass through the **Kopnena Vrata** (Land Gate), to the **Veliki Revelin Tower** bearing the Venetian coat of arms. The main street, ulica

Korčulanskog Statuta, leads to **St Mark's Cathedral** (020 711 049, open summer 8am-9pm daily, winter 8am-noon, 4-6.30pm daily), a fine example of local church architecture. Next door the **Abbey Treasury** (summer 9am-7pm daily, 10kn) has Dalmatian art from the 15th and 16th centuries.

The **Town Museum** (020 711 420, open 9am-1.30pm Mon-Sat, 10kn), set in a Venetian palace, has a copy of the fourth-century Greek tablet from Lumbarda, the earliest evidence of civilisation here.

Korčula's other hub is **Vela Luka**, the ferry port for Split, Hvar town and Lastovo. The **Culture Centre** (020 813 001, open summer 9am-noon, 6-10pm Mon-Sat, 6-10pm Sun, winter 9am-noon Mon-Sat, 10kn) here has two Henry Moores and archaeological finds from the nearby Vela Špilja cave, inhabited in Neolithic times.

From Korčula town, a regular 15-minute taxi boat runs to **Badija**, a lovely pine-forested island and haven for deer and naturists.

Getting there

A **bus** runs from Dubrovnik every day to Korčula town (3hrs, 80kn). Tickets include the ferry crossing.

Eating & drinking

Adio Mare

Ulica sv Roka (020 711 253). **Open** *Mid Apr-mid Oct* 6-11.30pm Mon-Sat; 6-11pm Sun. Closed Mid Oct-mid Apr. **Restaurant**.
Watch from the maritime-themed dining room as cooks in the open-plan kitchen flame-grill your fish or stew your beef in sherry and prunes, the famous house *pašticada*, served up with sticky gnocchi. Queues round the block in high season.

Massimo Cocktail Bar

Šetalište Petra Kanavelića (020 715 073). **Open** *May-Oct* 6pm-2am daily. Closed Nov-Apr. **Bar**. No credit cards.

Korčula's only real bar, Massimo is set under the turrets of the Zakerjan Tower in the fortifications. Cocktails (50kn) come to you by pulley as you take in a view as far as Pelješac.

Morski Konjić

Šetalište Petra Kanavelića (020 711 878). **Open** *Summer* 9am-1am daily. *Winter* 6pm-1am daily. **Restaurant**. The terrace Morski serves high-grade versions of local seafood favourites. Mussels are a rich starter but a light main, the grilled squid is a treat, and if you're having the *brodet*, fish stew, mind the bones. Round it off with the house *rakija* of figs and carob.

Mljet

Mljet is the nearest thing to having your own island. Some 70 per cent of this thin, 37km-long (22-mile) one-road idyll is pine forest. A third is **national park**. Mljet is an ideal escape, undeveloped and empty.

Tourists coming from Gruž by ferry arrive at **Sobra**, on the north coast. The catamaran also stops here, then to **Polače** in the west. The ticket for Polače is almost three times the price so if you're hiring a car, do so in Sobra (Mini Brum, 020 745 260, 098 285 566 mobile).

Between Polače and the new port of **Pomena** (with restaurants and the Mljet's only hotel, the seasonal Odisej, www.hotelodisej.hr) is the national park office at **Govedjari**. Kiosks are also dotted elsewhere. Entry includes a boat trip to the **Benedictine monastery**, set in the saltwaker lake of Veliko Jezero. You can hire a canoe and row there.

Few tourists venture further; the rest of Mljet is yours. From Veliko Jezera, a hiking path leads to the peak of **Montokuc**, with views of Pelješac and Korčula. Hiking maps (30kn) are sold at kiosks in Polače and Pomena. Other sports activities – windsurfing, diving – are run from the Odisej. Island capital

Babino Polje offers a great local bar, **Komarac**, and restaurant, **Triton**. Beyond is little but nature. Try and get to **Okuklje**, just east of Sobra – a tranquil, sheltered bay. At the far eastern tip are three sandy beaches near **Saplunara**. The main one can get busy, but the other two, **Podkućica** and **Blace**, are quieter, the latter for nudists. **Stermasi** provides a restaurant and apartments.

Getting there

The **Nona Ana** catamaran leaves Gruž at about 9am-10am daily. It stops at Sobra (26kn) then goes on to Polače (70kn). It turns round for Gruž in the mid-afternoon. The Jadrolinija **car ferry** from Gruž (2hrs; 32kn, cars 215kn) runs once a day, often in the afternoon, landing at Sobra. It turns around early the next day. The Dubrovnik-Bari line calls at Sobra thrice a week. A bus serves Sobra, Polače and Pomena according to ferry times – but it can be full in high season. There is no other public transport.

Sights & museums

Mljet National Park

Main office *Pristanište 2, Govedjari (020 744 041, www.np-mljet.hr).* **Open** *Apr-Oct* 24hrs daily. *Nov-Mar* 7am-3pm Mon-Fri. **Admission** *Summer* 90kn; 40kn concessions. *Winter* 60kn; 30kn concessions. No credit cards.
Mljet's main draw is this national park covering the western third of the island. Many first head for the salt-water lakes of Veliko and Malo Jezero, linked by a channel of water. Veliko Jezero is connected to the Adriatic and has tidal flows. In the centre is the islet of St Mary, with the church of the same name and a 12th-century monastery.

Eating & drinking

Komarac

Sršenovići 44, Babino Polje (no phone). **Open** 9am-midnight daily. **Bar**. No credit cards.

Božo Hadjić's Mosquito would grace any Adriatic isle – on empty Mljet, it's a godsend. A terrace with a verdant view adjoins a bar decorated with mosquitos: insects perched by coffee cups on the wall, framed war planes inside. Everyone from the island passes through, for a drink, a chat and a few drinks more. Decent rocky soundtrack.

Konoba Barba

Prožura (020 746 200/098 243 401 mobile/www.konoba-barba.hr). **Open** *Apr-Sept* 10am-midnight daily. Closed Oct-Apr. **Restaurant**. No credit cards. This is like dining in somebody's house, except that the house is set in a beautiful, protected bay a short hop from Sobra. There's even anchorage for yachts. Pizzas are the speciality here – try the house variety with chilli and anchovies.

Melita

St Mary's Island (020 744 145). **Open** *May-Sept* 10am-midnight daily. Closed Oct-Apr. **Restaurant**. No credit cards. A wonderful location, this, in the old monastery beneath the church on the islet in the middle of Veliko Jezero. You can sample pricier fish or grilled meats while dipping your toes in the water from the terrace. Melita is only accessed across the picturesque saltwater lake by boat or canoe.

Stermasi

Saplunara (098 939 0362 mobile/098 427 081 mobile/www.stermasi.hr). **Open** *Apr-Sept* 10am-midnight daily. Closed Oct-Mar. **Restaurant**. No credit cards. Set in pine trees overlooking the seafront at Saplunara. Octopus, goat and a rare vegetable-only mix are all slowly prepared *ispod peke*, under a cooking bell, for two. Allow two hours. There is also Mljet-style fish stew, a fish platter and sundry grills. Cheap year-round apartments also available.

Triton

Sršenovići 43, Babino Polje (020 745 131/091 205 3531 mobile). **Open** *Apr-Oct* 10am-midnight daily. Closed Nov-Mar. **Restaurant**. No credit cards. Rustic restaurant with a wonderful seaview terrace. Goat is the speciality, slow-cooked in hot coals – you can choose from octopus or veal too. Triton has a great range of own-made spirits – try the walnut variety.

Trsteno

Sights & museums

Arboretum

Trsteno (020 751 019). **Open** *May-Oct* 7am-7pm daily. *Nov-Apr* 8am-3pm. **Admission** 20kn. No credit cards.

Korčula p125

Arboretum

One of the main attractions in the region is set in a Renaissance villa, a graceful arboretum founded in the 16th century. The grounds, running down to the sea, are centrepieced by a grotto and baroque fountain.

Zaton Mali

Eating & drinking

Gverović-Orsan

Stikovića 43 (020 891 267/098 271 555 mobile/www.gverovic-orsan.hr). **Open** *Mar-Dec* noon-midnight Mon-Sat. Closed Jan, Feb. **Restaurant**.
This old boathouse is the best restaurant in the area, its terrace, beach (and shower) ideal for an aperitif or a dip before dining. Recommended is the house black risotto, four kinds of shells and shrimps sautéed in wine and lemon and mixed with rice soaked in black squid ink; perhaps prefaced by a milk-fish carpaccio, eaten whole with local olive oil. The motar salad is made from a plant that only grows on rocks by the sea. The 120-strong wine list includes a brand produced exclusively on Hvar for the restaurant.

Župa Dubrovačka

This string of coastal resorts 10km (six miles) south of town halfway to Cavtat is big with young locals. In summer the spots of **Srebreno – Club 22**, **Porto**, **Vertigo** – are packed. By day, the pebbly beaches of **Soline** and **Kupari** are busy, aided by the soft seabed ideal for games of **picigin**, a local version of keepie-uppie. The stone houses and pretty harbour of **Mlini** might suit the more relaxed visitor – but Župa Dubrovačka is about mindless fun. Regular buses from Dubrovnik for Cavtat all stop somewhere at Župa.

Eating & drinking

Club 22

Šetalište Franjo Tudjman, Srebreno (no phone). **Open** *Summer* noon-2am daily. **Bar**. No credit cards.
Beside Vertigo on the waterfront, Club 22 is the everyone's favourite pre-club bar, clearing out at 2am before the action moves next door.

Porto

Srebreno 6 (020 487 078). **Open** 7am-2am Mon-Thur, Sun; 7am-4am Fri, Sat. **Bar**. No credit cards.
This venue was popularised a couple of years before the scene started at the waterfront. Set in a car park, it's busy almost round the clock, all year round, with a traffic of trendy young things up for drinks and dancing. Live shows on Thursdays and Sundays, and DJs on Fridays and Saturdays, pack out the gallery and terrace in summer.

Vertigo

Šetalište Franjo Tudjman, Srebreno (020 487 540). **Open** *Summer* 7pm-late daily. **Bar**. No credit cards.
Calling itself a 'Caffe Night Bar', Vertigo is used as a club by locals piling in after nearby places close. Fifty kinds of cocktails, include a Vertigo (38kn) of white rum, Southern Comfort and fruit liqueurs, help lubricate the social interaction at the waterfront.

Essentials

Hotels

First things first. Croatia doesn't do the kind of simple, cheap, two- or three-star, family-run pension that is such a great feature of tourism in France, Spain or Portugal. When part of Yugoslavia, Croatia was a Communist country that had few Western guests until it decided in the 1960s to open itself up to package tourism.

When tour companies began flying holidaymakers to Dalmatia, Dubrovnik was accommodating movie stars on the luxury leisure circuit. While Richard and Liz were being lavished with opulence at the **Hotel Excelsior**, newly built resort hotels were springing up across the Lapad headland. Meanwhile, locals were exploiting a gap in the market by doing up the spare bedroom and renting it out to independent travellers.

Thus, when war broke out here in 1991, the accommodation stock could be divided three ways: luxury, package and private rooms. The destruction and near-decade disappearance of foreign tourists meant that Dubrovnik started the late 1990s from scratch. Despite the devastation, Dubrovnik didn't lose its cachet – film stars still came here to hang out, away from the overbearing glare of publicity prevalent elsewhere on the Med. The local Adriatic Luxury Hotel group saw the opportunity to invest a vast sum – more than €100 million – in rebuilding and upgrading hotels prominently placed around Dubrovnik. The former two-star **Bellevue** is a classic example. The **Hilton**, the **Pucić Palace**, the **Rixos Libertas** and other high-end hotels

Hilton Imperial p139

soon followed suit. In order to recoup their huge investments, companies are having to go for the €300-a-night market, with spa, pool and a fusion restaurant all de rigueur attractions. The result is a glut of five-star hotels.

Nearly all the package hotels have reopened, some available at a song to independent travellers in the shoulder season. Apart from the Pucić Palace and the **Hotel Stari Grad**, there are no hotels in the Old Town. A major development has been the growth and improvement of apartments for hire – if you're staying longer than three nights, and wish to be central, you're best looking into arranging lodging at the **Karmen apartments** or **Princess Dora**.

The private-room industry still thrives. Properties are inspected and officially approved then placed on a list of properties offered by tour agencies as part of their booking service. Alternatively,

ESSENTIALS

"I don't think I've ever drunk champagne before breakfast before. With breakfast on several occasions, but never before, before." BREAKFAST AT TIFFANY'S

ALH - reinventing passion

Home comforts

It's a perennial problem. You want to stay in the Old Town: the Pucić Palace is too pricy, the Hotel Stari Grad is full and a private room doesn't appeal. The solution? Marc van Bloemen's **Karmen apartments** (p135). You get location – so close to the old harbour one guest window overlooks it – plus comfort, convenience (modern kitchen, air-con and DVD) and character.

Few local hoteliers are more characterful than van Bloemen. Now in his forties, Marc was born and raised in the bohemian surroundings of the Troubadour café, a top folkie hangout in London's swinging '60s. He spent his boyhood peering over punters' heads to get a view of Donovan or Paul Simon. The travelling van Bloemens bought a place in Dubrovnik – the family album reflects a happy childhood spent in sunshine. When his parents decided to sell up, the rebellious teenager insisted on staying.

Educated in the Yugoslav state system, Marc did odd jobs in London to support himself. Kindly airport staff always found him a spare seat on a UK-bound plane. Bilingual and an adept handyman, he did up his folks' place, married local girl Silvia, and was making a life for himself when war broke out.

The day before the shelling, Marc moved his family to the UK. When they returned, his building skills were quickly put to good use. The ceiling in the airport bar, the tiling in the Pucić Palace, a renovated dining table in the Dubrovački kantun; all are Marc's handiwork. At the same time, he turned this house into four apartments. Today it's a convivial mix of arty bric-a-brac (an original Marcel Marceau self-portrait, a window of colourful glazed pebbles, a corridor lined with random framed old photographs) and the modern comforts you would find at a tidy four-star, with plenty of space to boot. Apartment no.1 has a view of the harbour, no.2 catches the morning sun. Your likeable host will leave you in peace, unless you're after a restaurant recommendation, a boat time or a local yarn.

rooms are hawked at the bus station by a legion of grandmothers who supplement their meagre pensions by exploiting the significant gap at the lower end of the market.

Timings and rates

Dubrovnik expects to make all its money in the high season. Hotels have been geared around trade in July and August, also expecting healthy occupancy rates in June and September. For several reasons, this trend is changing, although the local hotel trade has been slow to react. First, tourists from the UK are now arriving year-round thanks to a regular connection with London Gatwick. Secondly, visitors, in particular Italian visitors, have realised that Dubrovnik in August is unbearably crowded and seriously overpriced. In 2006, July was the busier month. Thirdly, Dubrovnik has been hit by its own perverse acceptance of cruise ships; up to three or four a day in high season. Not only do they hit the hotel trade, they hinder the all-important view of guests paying top dollar at the Excelsior and **Grand Villa Argentina**.

We have divided the hotels into four rack-rate price categories, according to the cost for one night in a double room with a shower: deluxe, €300 and over, **€€€€**; expensive, between €200 and €300, **€€€**; moderate, between €100 and €200, **€€**; cheap, up to €100, **€**. Most resort hotels close for the winter; many are booked solid by tour groups in summer.

Note that there is a universal rule of adding surcharges (about 20 per cent) on stays of less than three nights. Prices include a steep VAT rate levied by the government but not its nominal tourist tax.

Many hotels quote their rates per person, although we quote per room. Although we have divided our price brackets in euros, all venues accept local kunas or, in nearly every case, credit cards for payment. Breakfast is normally included. Many establishments offer half- and full-board options.

ESSENTIALS

Pucić Palace p137

Old Town

Apartments Nives

*Nikole Božidarevića 7 (020 323 181/
098 243 699 mobile/www.dubrovnik-
palace.com). €.*

Modest apartments in the Old Town,
ideal if you're not spending much time
indoors, somewhat cramped if you're
here during a rainy week. The larger of
the two apartments can (in theory)
sleep six, but would suit two couples.
There is considerably less space in the
smaller. Each has a kitchen, fridge and
washing machine. Another room has a
bed and bathroom. No arguing with the
price, €50 per apartment out of season,
nor with the central location.

Hotel Stari Grad

*Od Sigurate 4 (020 321 373/fax 020
321 256/www.hotelstarigrad.com). €€.*

After the Pucić Palace, the dinky Stari
Grad is the only other hotel choice in the
Old Town. It comprises eight quiet bedrooms, large enough for an extra bed
(250kn-400kn) if necessary, and a
panoramic fifth-floor roof terrace where
breakfast is served in summer. The
rooms are tastefully furnished but none

have a view. In winter you may find
yourself spending more time out of the
hotel than you would if you were spending the same money for a sea vista in
Lapad or Babin Kuk. Still, with half its
rooms for single travellers, and set only
a few minutes from the Pile Gate, the
Stari Grad is perfect for independent
visitors here to nose around the treasures of the Old Town.

Karmen apartments

*Bandureva 1 (020 323 433/098
619 282 mobile/www.karmendu.com).*
No credit cards. €€.

Surely the best bargain in Dubrovnik
– four comfortable apartments for hire
year-round at affordable prices not five
minutes' walk from the old harbour.
P133 **Home comforts**.

Princess Dora

*Žudioska 1 (020 321 143/098 170
561 mobile/www.dora-dubrovnik.com).*
No credit cards. €€.

Comfortable and convenient, cheaper
than many a hotel and convivial for a
couple, this top-floor attic apartment
overlooks Stradun. It comprises a bedroom, bathroom, a shiny new kitchen
and a dining room complete with a

six-seater table plus a huge leather sofa. Equipped with a large TV, DVD, fridge freezer and air-conditioning.

Pucić Palace

Od Puča 1 (020 326 200/fax 020 326 323/www.thepucicpalace.com). €€€€.
A beautifully crafted five-star in the heart of the Old Town, the stylish Pucić Palace combines old-world heritage with 21st-century convenience. The 19 individually and tastefully decorated rooms feature spacious bathrooms of Italian mosaic tiles, Egyptian cotton towels and thick bathrobes hanging on heated towel racks, with baroque-style furnishings in the bedrooms. Wi-Fi internet and DVD players provide technology; comfort comes from ample beds and sumptuous linens (choose your colour). Large, soundproofed windows allow views of the market scenes below – this former nobleman's pile faces prominent Gundulićeva poljana, which lends its name to the first-floor suite. On the roof terrace, the Defne restaurant (p63) is outstanding; the kitchen also serves the Razonada (p69) wine bar downstairs.

Ploče

Hotel Excelsior

Frana Supila 12 (020 353 353/fax 020 353 555/www.hotel-excelsior.hr). €€€.
Reopened at Easter 2007 after a major €3-million reconstruction. Now complemented by the adjacent boutique Villa Odak, the Excelsior is not only firing on all cylinders, but these recent developments echo its proud century-old history. Built by hotel owner Robert Odak in 1913, this villa complex became the Hotel Excelsior in 1930. Royals, Richard and Liz, and assorted Habsburgs all stayed here. In 1998 it became Croatia's first five-star hotel. The 154 bedrooms are tasteful and comfortable, relying on classic, understated luxury, rather than the flat-screen TVs and power showers in evidence elsewhere in town. Each of the 18 suites has a jacuzzi. The hotel has its own section of beach, outdoor pool for kids, indoor one for adults, gym and sauna. The Zagreb restaurant is classy, but perhaps the best feature is the palm terrace, ideal for a sunset drink. Yonder are the fortifications, Lokrum island and a backdrop of Adriatic blue. OK, not all rooms have a sea view, but this is five-star accommodation in the old-school style.

Hotel Grand Villa Argentina

Frana Supila 14 (020 440 555/fax 020 432 524/www.gva.hr). €€€.
This five-star villa-and-hotel complex has been ameliorated by the grand opening of the Villa Sheherezade. Behind its intricately renovated oriental façade, a banquet hall, two terraces and five luxury bedrooms with marble bathrooms accommodate up to a dozen people – all yours for a total of €6,000 a day. The price rating given above is for the two sister villas, both the Argentina and the Glavić, with beautifully appointed rooms, a little swimming pool, gym, sauna and terrace overlooking a wide stretch of private beach. The Villa Orsula and Hotel Argentina are slightly cheaper.

Villa Dubrovnik

Vlaha Bukovca 6 (020 422 933/fax 020 423 465/www.villa-dubrovnik.hr). Closed Oct-Mar. *€€€.*
Far enough away from the Old Town (1.5km/one mile) to warrant a handy complimentary boat service there and back five times a day, the summer-only Villa Dubrovnik allows tranquillity and isolation. Stunningly located over an accessible, secluded rocky outcrop lapped by the sea, all 40 rooms of the Villa Dubrovnik, set on descending terraces, have sea and Old-Town views, and all are beautifully appointed without many man-made amenities – hence the five-star prices for three-star status. The most attractive facility is the Bistro Giardino, a verdant, panoramic terrace and the ideal spot for a sunset cocktail before the last boat to town at 8.30pm. The rates in high season are for half-board only.

The latest in luxury

If you want to know about risk, talk to Goran Štrok. The man behind high-end Adriatic Luxury Hotels, now with three five-star properties, each at panoramic, vantage points in Dubrovnik, this former racing driver has invested some 100 million euros in the local tourist industry. Twenty million has just gone into the **Hotel Bellevue** (p141), officially opened on St Blaise's Day, February 2007.

Having worked as a consultant to major construction companies in the UK, Štrok moved into property development, buying the Bonavia Hotel in run-down Rijeka in 1995 while Croatia was still at war. Working with wife Renata, a notable painter and interior designer, they reopened it five years later as a four-star business hotel. The **Excelsior** in Dubrovnik was next revamped, then the ramshackle **Dubrovnik Palace** (since voted best hotel in Croatia at the World Travel Market) and now the old two-star Bellevue.

Built into the cliff face over five storeys (with private beach, sea-level grill restaurant and cocktail bar), the Bellevue is a showcase of engineering expertise – and the creative hand of Renata Štrok. A palm tree grows from the restaurant up to the reception area. Insistent on using domestic materials (olive wood, Dalmatian stone) and local contemporary artists (Željko Senečić, Dušan Djamonja and his son Fedor), Renata has given an imaginative, boutique touch to the lobby, the cinema screening room, the Vapor restaurant and adjoining Spice Lounge bar, the spa and kidney-shaped panoramic pool – but most of all, to the 93 rooms.

Each has a dramatic sea view, all but five boast a large balcony, whose partitioning use of glass is echoed in the bathrooms. Wood, stone and tastefully selected furniture feature throughout.

The entrance stands on the busy Iva Vojnovića road linking Lapad to the Old Town three bus stops or ten minutes' walk away. Within, high above Danče Bay, all is calm.

With the high-end apartments in the adjacent Villa Miramare opening spring 2007, the Bellevue looks set to rival any of the best five-star hotels around the Med.

Pile & Boninovo

Hilton Imperial

Marijana Blažića 2 (020 320 320/fax 020 320 220/www.hilton.co.uk/ Dubrovnik). €€€€.

Swish and business-like, the Hilton's first operation in Croatia was launched in 2005. Occupying a grand, caramel-coloured, fin-de-siècle building set in from the sea and a short walk from the Pile Gate, it has location without the beachside grace of other five-star establishments in town. With its gym and indoor pool open 24 hours, this is the place for execs to convene. They have their own fourth-floor lounge, and can make use of five meeting rooms, three ballrooms for presentations and exhibitions, a boardroom and business centre. And the bedrooms? Simple, modern with large beds, they are comfortable but unmemorable, many standard ones without sea views. The Porat restaurant (p97) provides stand-out Mediterranean cuisine, the lobby bar has a panoramic terrace and the pool is flooded with natural light.

Gruž

Hotel Petka

Obala Stjepana Radića 38 (020 410 500/fax 020 410 127/www.croatia-vacation.com). €.

A convenient place to flop after that long bus or ferry journey, the three-star Petka now has a few extras after its recent upgrade. Most of the 100-plus rooms have a balcony overlooking Gruž bay and harbour, and access to a gym and good restaurant (p102). The full-board supplement is a snip.

Lapad

Begović Boarding House

Primorska 17 (020 435 191/fax 020 452 752). €.

A budget favourite located on a street parallel but high up over šetalište kralja Zvonimira in Lapad. Old man Begović will meet you at the harbour or bus station and take you, perhaps via a little sightseeing tour of Dubrovnik, up to your quarters. OK, they're just private rooms and you'll have to make do with shared bathrooms, but it's cheap as chips (about €15 a head), the couple are sweethearts and the back terrace is a boon.

Grand Hotel Park

Šetalište kralja Zvonimira 39 (020 434 444/fax 020 434 886/www.grandhotel-park.hr). Closed Nov-Mar. €€.

A large, landmark tourist hotel set just behind Lapad beach. In fact, the Park comprises more than the eight-floor monolith overlooking the headland – two four-star stone villas stand adjacent, their rooms in the same price range. All 150-plus rooms in the main hotel have a balcony, half have a sea view. There are two sea-water pools; the chic indoor one is heated. A sauna and massage treatments complete the attractions – sadly, the rather splendid, British-owned Konoba Barun downstairs folded in the winter of 2006-07. Easy walk to the beach.

Hotel Adriatic

Masarykov put 9 (020 433 520/fax 020 433 530/www.hotelimaestral.com). Closed early Nov-mid Mar. €.

Simple, cheap, holiday two-star in the Maestral group set between greenery and the edge of Lapad beach. The Adriatic's functional 158 rooms are filled with undemanding, younger holidaymakers happy to spend a week taking advantage of the water sports on offer, the tennis court and the beach. Internet facility too.

Hotel Argosy

Iva Dulčića 41 (052 465 000/fax 020 435 622/www.valamar.com). Closed Dec-Mar. €€.

Recently taken under the umbrella of the Valamar group, the Argosy has enjoyed a winter of renovation. Its Lindjo restaurant now leads down to the pool, so guests can enjoy breakfast or dinner (half-board rates are most reasonable) with a view, even designating their table from the off. It's a

ESSENTIALS

Hotel Lero

TAVERNA
NAVA

tradicionalna
dalmatinska kuhinja
traditional
dalmatian kitchen

11:00 - 24.00
reservation/tel: 332 581

hotel Lero
DUBROVNIK - CROATIA

Our personalities are a reflection of our point of view.
Timelessness is a trait of God.

The perfect holiday is a combination of both!

IMPORTANNE RESORT DUBROVNIK
Hotel Neptun | Hotel Ariston | Importanne Suites | Villa Elita

Phone: +385 20 440 100
info@importanneresort.com | www.importanneresort.com

family-friendly place, tucked in behind the Dubrovnik President, with access to the Cava beach and use of tennis courts, plus two pools, one for children. There are kids' activities in the summer. The standard three-star rooms are comfortable enough, all have balconies, some with sea views. In spring and autumn you can get a basic double with breakfast for under €100.

Hotel Bellevue
Pera Čingrije 7 (020 330 000/fax 020 330 100/www.hotel-bellevue.hr). **€€**.
Opened on St Blaise's Day in February 2007, a major feat of engineering and the last word in upscale relaxation, not 15 minutes' walk from the Old Town. P138 **The latest in luxury**.

Hotel Dubrovnik
Šetalište kralja Zvonimira (020 435 030/fax 020 435 999/www.hotel dubrovnik.hr). **€€**.
The year-round Dubrovnik, its white façade set by the Hotel Perla halfway down the main drag to Lapad beach, is a standard resort three-star. Signature walk-round balconies and the terrace restaurant below catch the sun. The extra star and €160-a-night price tag for an air-conditioned double in summer attract a slightly higher class of tourist. Room service until 10pm is another plus. Out of season, you can get something for €75.

Hotel Dubrovnik Palace
Masarykov put 20 (020 430 000/ fax 020 430 100/www.dubrovnik palace.hr). **€€€**.
Until the recent arrival of sister hotel the Bellevue (see above), this superbly equipped flagship of the Adriatic Luxury Hotels group was top dog in Dubrovnik. Croatia's best hotel at the World Travel Market in 2005 and 2006, the Dubrovnik Palace opened in 2004 after a lengthy renovation. The result is a ten-floor, 308-room luxury hotel equally suited to commercial travellers and tourists. Business is done in the well-equipped conference and meeting rooms. The pleasure is in the setting; the original designer Vincek placed the Palace in a tangle of woodland paths at the south-west tip of Lapad, looking out to the Elafiti islands. That was in 1972. This is what everyone still sees from their balcony, from the 11 bars, three restaurants, four pools and the fitness centre. Even the 234 standard rooms are spacious, each with flat-screen TVs, internet access and a laptop; all have been touched by the creative hand of renowned designer Renata Štrok. The main presidential suite, one of two, is the size of a small house. The off-season rates (early Jan-late Mar) compare favourably with the price of a boxy three-star in London. In high season, your budget may not stretch to prices at twice that rate, but any visitor is welcome to a drink in the panoramic Sunset Lounge (p118). In fact, it's obligatory.

Hotel Dubrovnik President
Iva Dulčića 39 (052 465 000/fax 020 435 622/www.valamar.com). **€€€**.
The leading lodging of the Valamar group, this one ruled the roost on the Babin Kuk headland until the Dubrovnik Palace (see left) came along. Set right on the western tip, it commands its own section of beach, and each of the 181 rooms has a balcony view of the sea and Elafiti islands beyond. In essence, it's a high-end resort hotel, with an indoor pool, children's entertainment and playground, and access to nearby tennis courts. If turning up on spec, for these rates you're better off in the Dubrovnik Palace – unless you're with the kids.

Hotel Ivka
Put Sv Mihajla 21 (020 362 600/ 020 362 660/www.hotel-ivka.com). **€€**.
More pleasant than the dreary picture on its website suggests, the newly opened Ivka is a standard year-round three-star set near the twin churches of St Michael in the heart of the Lapad headland. Two restaurants turn out decent Dalmatian cuisine (there are attractive half-board deals as well), the sea is 15 minutes' walk away and autumn rates fall below €80.

Hotel Komodor

Masarykov put 5 (020 433 500/fax 020 433 510/www.hotelimaestral.com). Closed early Nov-mid Mar. €€€.

It's almost as old as the local tourist industry, this sturdy stone hotel, part of the Maestral cluster, just set in from Lapad beach. It's a three-star, thanks mainly to the popular outdoor pool, but it's a nice size, the service is a little friendlier and you often get regulars coming back every summer. Appeals to a more adult crowd.

Hotel Kompas

Šetalište kralja Zvonimira 56 (020 352 000/fax 020 435 877/www.hotel-kompas.hr). €€.

Formerly a standard package-tour hotel which has since been taken over by the Adriatic Luxury Hotels group (note the fragrant Gharani Štrok soap in the bathroom). The refurbished Kompas and its expansive terrace restaurant overlook Lapad beach. Now equipped with a modest sauna, gym, indoor sea-water pool, outdoor pool (complete with a lido bar) and even conference facilities, the Kompas remains a good, reasonably priced choice for families in the shoulder months. Half the 115 rooms have a balcony with a sea view – the rate climbs just over €200 in high season. There are also tennis courts nearby.

Hotel Lapad

Lapadska obala 37 (020 432 922/ fax 020 417 230/www.hotel-lapad.hr). Closed Nov-Mar. €€.

Overlooking the Gruž harbour waterfront, this well-known three-star consists of three elements: a fin-de-siècle façade facing the main road towards the Babin Kuk headland, containing the lobby and reception area; and, the other side of an outdoor pool and a pleasant courtyard, the accommodation building divided into two wings. Of the nearly 200 rooms, the ones in the older wing are cheaper. The Lapad still has a taste of times gone by, with an on-site hairdresser, as well as pool parties and musical entertainment in

the summer. Handy for Lapad and the Old Town, and a ten-minute walk from the ferry port and bus station.

Hotel Lero

Iva Vojnovića 14 (020 341 333/fax 020 332 133/www.hotel-lero.hr). €€.

The advantages of this Socialist-style, 152-room hotel are location and price. Equidistant between the Old Town and the main bus station and ferry terminal at Gruž, the three-star Lero offers simple, comfortable rooms, half with a sea view, a surprisingly extensive buffet breakfast and attractive full-board deals all year round at the traditional adjoining Taverna Nava. And it's only a short walk to the sheltered stretch of beach on the other side of the bay from the Pile Gate.

Hotel Neptun

Kardinala Alojzija Stepinca 31 (020 440 100/fax 020 440 200/www.hotel-neptun.hr). €€.

This former Socialist-style holiday hotel has been completely overhauled and opens in 2007 as part of a four-property seafront leisure complex. P145 Importanne Resort.

Hotel Perla

Šetalište kralja Zvonimira (020 438 244/fax 020 438 245/www.perla-dubrovnik.com). €€.

A simple little 20-room hotel set back from the busy pedestrianised street leading down to Lapad beach. With the bright terrace of the Agora attracting passers-by, the Perla looks much grander from the outside, its pretty balconies all lending it a chalet-like appearance. The bedrooms are standard, although you're really paying for the location. Disabled access.

Hotel R

Alberta Hallera 2 (020 333 200/ fax 020 333 208/www.hotel-r.hr). Closed Nov-Feb. €€.

A basic but by no means uncomfortable three-star near the Hotel Lero, at the Montovjerna end of Lapad, built in 2001. It's equidistant between Lapad beach and the Old Town, which means

Grandma knows best

It's a familiar sight and one that won't go away the more that high-end hotels sprout up in Dubrovnik. You pull into Gruž bus station or harbour. Surrounding you is a gaggle of grandmothers waving signs and chanting the mantra written thereupon: 'Rooms, rooms!'

The unregistered private room industry thrives in Dubrovnik due to the dearth of budget beds and a lack of hotels in the Old Town. Gruž is a steep trek and after a bone-jarring five-hour bus ride from Split, the last thing any backpack-hauling traveller needs is a climb in the burning sun to an unknown warren of tourist-swamped streets to find digs. Ring any door bearing a blue plaque with a bed sign and the word *sobe* ('rooms') – chances are the one bedroom is taken. The hotel hub, Lapad, is an expansive headland where rooms are often block-booked in summer anyway. The budget bed-seeker's odds improve along pedestrianised šetalište kralja Zvonimira towards Lapad beach, but the high-season charge is 100 euros minimum.

Ergo: grandmother. You follow the old lady, her limited German communicating the promise of 'a room, very good, come come'. Ideally you come come to a standard bedroom furnished c1964, with easy access to a clean, shared bathroom and, most importantly, well located. Yours for €40. Judge and inspect first – you're under no obligation to take a shoebox in Nuncijata.

You'll be occupying the bedroom of a family member, someone married off or working abroad. All will be dusted and tidy – this is granny's livelihood. The sheets will be clean, a thin towel provided. Cash and keys are exchanged.

To save time and skirt the Nuncijata factor, go to a travel agency for approved and inspected lodging. Atlas by the Pile Gate (p154) is as good as any. There is a modest registration fee and tourist tax but you get the key and photocopied map right away. Contact with the hosts is minimal. Some may also prefer to give their kuna to a crone with a tale to tell.

you'll be relying on buses for either. For price, though, you can't beat it, the rates only going into three figures from June to September, with supplements for short stays and balcony provision. The R caters for single travellers, with two cheapish rooms, and there's also a triple at about €50 a head in summer. Half-board also available.

Hotel Splendid

Masarykov put 10 (020 433 560/fax 020 433 570/www.hotelimaestral.com). Closed early Nov-mid Mar. €€

A more enticing resort hotel, this, thanks to its sea-facing location and verdant surroundings. All the same, for three months of the year it's a honeycomb of holidaymakers, who swarm the adjoining tennis court and little beach. The Glorijet restaurant does a decent job of Dalmatian standards, some dishes slow-cooked under hot coals. So far, so conventional – but you'll be writing postcards home about the stunning sunsets.

Hotel Sumratin

Šetalište kralja Zvonimira 31 (020 436 333/fax 020 436 006/www.hotels-sumratin.com). Closed Nov-mid Mar. €.

Twinned with the nearby Hotel Zagreb, the 44-room Sumratin has the same convenient location – a stroll to Lapad beach, away from the crowds and with a bus stop to the Old Town round the corner – at just over half the price. If you're intending to spend most of the time outdoors, then this modest, clean lodging is a low-cost possibility.

Hotel Uvala

Masarykov put 6 (020 433 580/fax 020 433 590/www.hotelimaestral.com). Closed early Nov-mid Mar. €€.

The newest, best designed and only four-star of the Maestral group clustered here, the Uvala boasts a decent and spacious spa centre with aromatherapy and massage treatments, indoor and outdoor pools, a steam room, sauna and solarium. Its Mantala restaurant offers guests Dalmatian and macrobiotic meals, while the Rozolin bar provides imaginative spirit mixes.

Hotel Vis

Masarykov put 4 (020 433 555/fax 020 433 550/www.hotelimaestral.com). Closed early Nov-mid Mar. €€.

Standard resort hotel of 150 rooms spread around a sandy beach, presided over by a sea-facing bar and restaurant. If that's what you're after, you're in business – and in June you'll find a double with balcony here at just over €100. In high season there'll be entertainment laid on – peace and quiet will be at a premium.

Hotel Zagreb

Šetalište kralja Zvonimira 27 (020 438 930/fax 020 436 006/www.hotels-sumratin.com). Closed Nov-early Mar. €€.

Set in its own pleasant grounds in from the main drag through Lapad down to the beach nearby, the Zagreb has recently gained an extra star. Once installed in one of its homely 23 rooms, you'll see why: the back garden and terrace provide some much needed respite from the holiday swarms, with floodlit tennis courts on hand. Buses for the Old Town stop nearby and half-board rates are a reasonable extra. The nearby Hotel Sumratin is under the same management.

Importanne Resort

Kardinala Alojzija Stepinca 31 (020 440 100/fax 020 440 200/www.hotel-neptun.hr). €€.

Opening in the spring of 2007, this ambitious recreation complex on the edge of the Lapad headland comprises four elements: two overhauled holiday hotels, the Neptun and the Ariston; and two upscale properties, the Importanne Suites and the Villa Elita. The price codes above refer to a double (luxury or panoramic, there's nothing much 'standard' any more) in one of the hotels in high season – a couple can find one at under €100 by the autumn. There may be an LCD TV in every room, but a 300-room resort hotel is still a 300-room resort hotel. There's a fifth element, of course, nature: the Blue Flag beach and the pine trees all

ESSENTIALS

around. The facilities (massage rooms, hydromassage showers, two outdoor seawater pools) are the shape of things to come in Dubrovnik – as is the €400 price tag on the suites in summer.

Rixos Hotel Libertas

Liechtensteinov put 3 (020 333 720/fax 020 333 723/www.rixos.com). **€€€**.
Scheduled to open in the summer of 2007, the Libertas should be the last word in five-star luxury in Dubrovnik. The renovation of this landmark tourist hotel, devastated by the bombardment of 1991, has seen this far side of Danče Bay festooned with cranes for three years. Nearby stands the newly opened Hotel Bellevue (p141), competition that the Turkish-owned Rixos group has invested some €50 million in beating. Fourteen sea-facing floors will contain 300 rooms, 17 suites, a spa, a gym, pools indoors and out, three restaurants including a sushi bar, a casino, nightclub and 1,000-seater congress hall. Oh, and the largest hotel lobby in Europe. The Libertas does seem to tick every box but will need to pitch its prices carefully if it is to maintain occupancy rates in the low season.

Solitudo

Iva Dulčića 34 (020 448 686/fax 020 448 688/www.valamar.com). Closed Nov-Mar. **€**.
Dubrovnik's only campsite is set in five hectares of leafy space with capacity for 280 pitches, in the middle of the Lapad headland. It has its own shops, restaurant and stretch of beach. Campers can use the two pools (adults' and children's) at the nearby Tirena Hotel (see below), also in the Valamar group, as well as their tennis courts.

Tirena Hotel

Iva Dulčića 22 (052 465 000/fax 020 435 622/www.valamar.com). Closed Nov-Apr. **€€**.
Renovated in 2006, the summer-only Tirena shares the sports and recreational facilities with the other nearby Valamar hotels in the group: tennis courts, children's playground, pools for kids and adults, a programme of entertainment for youngsters and easy access to the beach. It's three-star, so prices are reasonable even if the rooms are pretty functional. They charge less than €100 in the off-season.

Valamar Club Dubrovnik

Iva Dulčića 18 (052 465 000/fax 020 435 622/www.valamar.com). Closed Dec-Mar. **€€**.
The perfect choice for families, the former Minčeta is now a rather bright new member of the Valamar group. Recreation is the key here. Set in its own patch of woodland, the Valamar Club Dubrovnik is also the one nearest to the Copacabana beach, with its water chutes, banana rides and pedalos. The hotel has a large, outdoor pool, children's pool and a full summer programme for kids. Many of the 300-plus rooms have a sea view. The venue shares its ample sports facilities – a dozen tennis courts, a small football pitch, mini-golf and a sea diving centre – with the other hotels in the group that are located nearby.

Valamar Lacroma Resort

Iva Dulčića 34 (020 448 234/fax 020 435 622/www.valamar.com). **Opening 2008.** **€€€**.
The largest conference and spa hotel in Dubrovnik will open its doors in 2008. Nearly 400 rooms, half with a sea view, will be complemented by a cluster of meeting rooms, treatment salons and saunas, two restaurants, four bars and three pools. Executive pampering is the name of the game here – the presidential suite is the size of a large apartment and the executive spa will put most facilities in town to shame.

Vila Micika

Mata Vodopića 10 (020 437 332/fax 020 437 323/www.vilamicika.hr). **€**.
Cheap and well positioned, albeit with quite compact rooms, the year-round two-storey Micika attracts a significant number of Japanese tourists. Perhaps it's the price (singles at €20 in winter!), perhaps it's the proximity of the Lapad tennis courts. There are also a pair of triples. The rates quoted are without

Hotel Kompas p142

Valamar Club Dubrovnik p146

breakfast, which costs €8 extra, or there are plenty of cafés nearby on the main path down to the beach.

Villa Rašica

Ivanska 14 (020 438 900/fax 020 438 921/www.villa-rasica.com). Closed Nov-Apr. €.

Prices vary at this bungalow complex leading down to Lapad beach, but expect to pay about €40 or €50 per head, plus a modest supplement for breakfast. High stone walls separate the compound from the holiday buzz of Lapad, so relative tranquillity is assured if you're after some privacy. Leafy paths link the properties and the owners keep a tight ship – all in all, a very pleasant experience.

Villa Wolff

Šetalište Niki i Meda Pucića 1 (020 438 710/fax 020 356 432/www.villa-wolff.hr). Closed Nov-Mar. €€.

Calling itself a 'boutique & beach hotel', the Villa Wolff is small (only six rooms, none really boutique) but certainly comfortable and indubitably by the beach. As the name suggests, it's also a converted villa, owned by the Wolff family, who in turn converted it from a monastery. Managed by the wonderfully named Gonzales Wolff, it comprises three double rooms, one small suite and two larger ones with balconies. The Wolffs have seen fit to give them all Greek names. The sea-view setting is lovely and the high-speed internet access in every room is certainly a bonus – but the Villa Wolff is simply a more palatable alternative to the large-scale resort hotels nearby. Do watch out for the hefty hikes for short-term stays. The popular Casa Bar (p111) downstairs doubles up as the hotel restaurant.

YH Dubrovnik

Vinka Sagrestana 3/bana Josipa Jelačića 15-17 (020 423 241/fax 020 412 592/www.hfhs.hr). €.

A clean and comfortable year-round youth hostel, located equidistant between the Old Town, Gruž bus station and harbour, and the seaside attractions of Lapad. It's also beside a strip of bars including the rather marvellous Roxy (p117). It provides 14 four-bedded rooms, four six-bedded dorms, plus one double. Prices range from €11 per head for a simple bed to €20 for half-board in the high season. A simple breakfast is included and there are kitchen facilities downstairs. Watch out for the 2am curfew.

Getting Around

Arriving & leaving

By air

Dubrovnik airport

Čilipi (020 773 377/020 773 233/www. airport-dubrovnik.hr). Some 22km (13 miles) south east of Dubrovnik.

Direct flights to Dubrovnik from the UK take just under three hours. As well as the two national carriers, British Airways and Croatia Airlines, low-cost and charter companies flybe and Thomsonfly have a direct UK service. There are currently no direct flights from the United States to Croatia.

Buses (30mins, 30kn) meet incoming flights, stopping in town near the Pile Gate before going on to the main bus station in Gruž. This is also the site of the main **ferry terminal**. From town, buses leave bay nos.6-8 at the station two hours before flights on British Airways and other foreign carriers, 90 minutes before Croatia Airlines ones. They also stop at the old bus station halfway to the Old Town, then at a municipal bus stop on the main road just north of the Old Town, opposite the shop Oleviri Logorio. This is the nearest jump-on point from the centre of town.

A **taxi** to town costs about 250kn, probably nearer to 350kn if you're staying at a hotel located on the Lapad or Babin Kuk headland. You can call one on 970. **Niksa** (00 385 91 531 0022 mobile) is also recommended.

British Airways

UK office *0870 850 9850/ www.britishairways.com.* **Dubrovnik office** *020 773 212.* **Open** 10am-5pm daily. Flies from London Gatwick.

Croatia Airlines

UK office *020 8563 0022.* **Croatia office** *01 487 27 27/ www.croatiaairlines.hr.* Flies from London Heathrow.

flybe

0871 522 6100/www.flybe.com Flies from Birmingham.

Thomsonfly

0870 190 0737/www.thomsonfly.com Flies from London Gatwick, London Luton and Manchester.

By boat

Croatia is accessible from Italy by sea. The main route to Dubrovnik is via Bari, the service calling at Hvar, Split and Rijeka.

Croatia's main passenger line is Jadrolinija (051 666 111, www.jadrolinija.hr). Other companies operating routes to and from Croatia include SEM Marina (www.sem-marina.hr) and Italian companies such as Adriatic (www.adriatica.it), Sanmar (www.sanmar.it) and Tirrenia (www.tirrenia.it).

By rail

Dubrovnik has no train station. The nearest main station is in Split, with an InterCity link to Zagreb. From there, to reach Dubrovnik you must drive or catch a bus (4.5 hours, about 120kn).

Information on rail links between Croatia and other countries, as well as on internal routes, can be found from Croatian Railways (060 333 444, www.hznet.hr).

By bus

Eurolines run a service from London to Split and Sarajevo – but not as far as Dubrovnik. Of the national Croatian bus companies serving Dubrovnik, AutoTrans (www.autotrans.hr) is the main one.

By road

Croatia's road system is improving dramatically, with many major motorway constructions underway or recently completed. The most notable is the motorway between Zagreb and Split, opened in 2005.

The rules of the road are stringent: seat belts must be worn front and rear, and using a mobile while driving is forbidden. No under-12s are allowed in the front seat. You must always drive with your lights on. Croatia has **zero tolerance** to drink driving – you can have no booze at all before you get in your car.

The **speed limit** is 50km/hr (30mph) in built up areas, 90km/hr (56mph) outside built up areas, 110km/hr (70mph) on major motor routes designed for motor vehicles, and 130km/hr (80mph) on motorways. In the event of an accident, contact the police on **92**.

English-language traffic reports are given on radio HR2 throughout the day. Updates are also posted on the website of the Croatian Automobile Club (01 464 0800, www.hak.hr).

Car hire

Car hire in Croatia is expensive – about 500kn a day for an average family car. Try and get some quotes online before you travel to avoid any nasty surprises when you arrive. Rental requirements are that drivers must be over 21 and must have held their driving licence for at least one year.

The following car hire companies operate from Dubrovnik:
Avis Dubrovnik airport & **central** 020 773 811/091 314 3010 mobile/ www.avis.com.
Hertz Dubrovnik airport & **central** 020 425 000/www.hertz.hr.
Thrifty Car Rental Dubrovnik airport 020 773 588/www.subrosa.hr.

Parking

Parking is not difficult – just dear. You pay by the hour, sometimes up to 30kn. Don't be tempted to park where you shouldn't (or arrive too late back to collect the car) – the local *pauk* ('spider'), or tow van, will whisk your car to the pound, leaving you with a journey across town and a bill of 500kn. Check if your hotel offers parking or drive to a free zone and walk back.

Bringing your own car

To enter Croatia by car you need a valid driving licence with a photograph, vehicle registration documents and insurance documents (with a Green Card).

City transport

Buses

A network of **Libertas buses** link Gruž, Babin Kuk, Lapad and Ploče to the Old Town. Buy a ticket (8kn) from any newsstand or Libertas kiosk, or from the driver on board (10kn). Day passes (25kn) are sold at Libertas kiosks. Buses run from about 6am to midnight – there is no night service. The main hub is by the Pile Gate on Brsalje.

Taxis

Taxis start at 25kn and charge 8kn per kilometre. Expect to pay 70kn from the rank on Brsalje to the harbour or bus station at Gruž. You can call on one 970.

Walking & bicycle

Cycling for tourists is growing, as is mountain biking – **Adriatic Kayak Tours** (p99) lays on trips. **Cicerone** (www.cicerone.co.uk) publishes *Walking In Croatia*; **Sunflower** (www.sunflowerbooks. co.uk) issues the hiking guide *Landscapes of Croatia*.

Resources A-Z

Accident & emergency

Croatia's reciprocal agreement with the UK means that British passport holders are entitled to free hospital treatment in Croatia. Even so, we do recommend investing in travel insurance. The general standard of care in Croatia is good. Your best bet is to go to the local hospital or emergency unit where a duty doctor can have a look at you.

Dubrovnik Hospital

Roka Misetica, Lapad (020 431 777). Dubrovnik's main hospital is some 4km (2.4 miles) from the Old Town.

Emergency numbers

Call 92 for the police, 93 for the fire brigade and 94 for an ambulance.

Credit card loss

American Express

Croatia office *01 612 4422.* **Emergencies** *01 612 4400.* *www.americanexpress.com* This office is in Zagreb. If calling on a foreign mobile from Dubrovnik, dial 00 385 1, then the next seven digits.

Diners Club

Croatia office *01 480 2333.* **Emergencies** *0800 11 44.* *www.dinersclub.com*

Mastercard

Emergencies *00 1 636 722 7111.* *www.mastercard.com/hr* Mastercard has no office or number in Croatia. For enquiries from Croatia, you have to call the 24-hour American number listed above.

Visa

Emergencies *866 654 0125.* *www.visa.com*

Customs

Foreign currency can be taken freely in and out of the country, and local currency up to an amount of 15,000kn. You are permitted 200 cigarettes or cigarillos or 50 cigars or 250g of tobacco, and one litre of spirits, two litres of liqueur or dessert or sparkling wine and two litres of table wine. Valuable professional and technical equipment needs to be declared at the border. It must leave with you again – you should not sell it while you're in Croatia.

Any cultural artefact, art or archaeological find can only be exported with necessary approval. For information see www.carina.hr.

Dental emergencies

Check with Dubrovnik Hospital (*see left*) for details.

Disabled

Croatia is not as enlightened as other countries in providing facilities for disabled people. That is changing as a result of the large number of people left handicapped by the fighting in the 1990s.

Make enquiries with your hotel as to whether it has disabled access and facilities – a number of hotels do, but certainly not all.

For more information, check with the Croatian Association of Organisations of Disabled Persons, www.soih.hr.

Electricity

Croatia uses a 220V, 50Hz voltage and continental two-pin plugs. UK visitors require an adaptor.

ESSENTIALS

Embassies & Consulates

These national offices are all in Zagreb. Dial 00 385 1 then the last seven digits if you're calling on a foreign mobile phone in Dubrovnik.

Australian Embassy

01 48 91 200/www.auembassy.hr. **Open** 8.30am-4.30pm Mon-Fri.

British Embassy

01 60 09 100/british.embassyzagreb@ fco.gov.uk. **Open** 8.30am-5pm Mon-Thur; 8.30am-2pm Fri.
Consulate *Obala Hrvatskog Narodnog Preporoda 10/III, Split (021 346 007/ british-consulat-st@st.htnet.hr).*

Canadian Embassy

01 48 81 200. **Open** 8am-noon, 1.30-3pm Mon-Fri.

Irish Honorary Consul

01 63 10 025/irish. consulate.zg@ inet.hr). **Open** 8am-noon, 2-3pm Mon-Fri.

New Zealand Consulate

01 61 51 382. **Open** 8am-noon, 1.30-3pm Mon-Fri.

US Embassy

01 66 12 200/www.usembassy.hr. **Open** 8am-noon, 1.30-3pm Mon-Fri.

Internet

Ante Starčićeva 7 (020 427 591/ www.tzdubrovnik.hr). **Open** *July, Aug* 8am-midnight daily. *June, Sept* 8am-10pm daily. *Oct-May* 9am-9pm Mon-Fri; 9am-7pm Sat.
In the same room as the main tourist office near the Pile Gate, this office has enough space for a dozen or so computers at reasonable hourly rates.
Netcafé Prijeko 21 (020 321 025/ www.netcafe.hr). **Open** *Summer* 9am-1am daily. *Winter* 9am-11pm daily.
Pricy but convenient place in the Old Town. It has plenty of computers and serves decent coffee. You can also scan, print, fax and connect your own laptop.

Money

The unit of Croatian currency is the kuna (kn). Coins are for 1, 2 and 5kn, notes for 5, 10, 20, 50, 100, 200, 500 and 1,000kn.

Euros are accepted in some hotels, and shops and restaurants in town – but the currency in everyday use is the kuna.

Foreign currency can be exchanged in banks, post offices, most tourist agencies, bureaux de change and at some hotels. ATMs and credit card use are widespread.

Opening hours

Public sector offices and most businesses usually work from 8am to 4pm Monday to Friday. Post offices are open from 7am to 7pm, and generally close at weekends. Shops open from 8am to 8pm weekdays and until 2pm or 3pm on Saturdays, although in summer some stay open much longer.

Banks are usually open 7am-7pm Monday to Friday.

Pharmacies

Kod Zvonika

Stradun (020 321 133). **Open** 7am-8pm Mon-Fri; 7.30am-8pm Sat.
Located in the Old Town, this is the main late-opening chemist.

Police

See p151.

Post

Post office

Put republike 32 (020 413 960/ www.posta.hr). **Open** 7am-8pm Mon-Fri; 8am-4pm Sat; 8am-noon Sun.
Between the Old Town and Gruž, this is the main post office. One branch is closer to the Old Town at Ante Starčićeva 2 (open 8am-3pm Mon-Fri).

ESSENTIALS

Safety

Croatia has a low rate of street crime. Foreign women may not appreciate attention they get from local men, especially in coastal areas. If it's in danger of crossing the line between flirtation and harrassment don't be shy of making your displeasure known.

Landmines

Landmines are a problem in the countryside. Look out for signs bearing a skull and crossbones and stay well clear. However, not all minefields are marked and it is definitely not advisable to wander around any abandoned villages or across uncultivated fields. Around Dubrovnik this problem concerns Mount Srdj just outside town – always stick to the footpath.

Smoking

A large proportion of Croats smoke and it is a far more socially acceptable habit than in the UK or US. Very few restaurants, cafés and bars have a no-smoking area. Smoking is not permitted in public buildings and cinemas, and on public transport.

Telephones

The dialling code for Croatia is +385. Croatian town and city codes have a zero in front of them that must left off when calling from overseas. When calling overseas from Croatia, the prefix 00 is the international access code. The code for Dubrovnik is 020.

Public phones

Public telephones use cards bought from post offices and kiosks. They come in units ('*impulsa*') from 25 to 500. Units run down fast calling internationally and you need a card of at least 50 *impulsa*, which should cost about 50kn.

It may be more convenient to place a call from a booth set up at most post offices.

Mobile phones

Croatia relies on the mobile. Roaming agreements exist with foreign companies and if you have a roaming facility on your mobile, the only problem should be the hideous expense.

An alternative is to purchase a local SIM card with a pre-paid subscription; you can usually buy a card with some starter airtime, although you should make sure your mobile is unlocked. If you're only in Croatia for a short while, you may need to buy top-up vouchers at a cost of 50kn or 100kn.

Time

Croatia is on Central European Time, GMT +1.

Tipping

Tipping is expected by taxi drivers and waiters in restaurants. Round up bills to the next 10kn-20kn, or by about ten per cent.

You don't tip in cafés, unless you have received special service or have been there for a while.

Tourist information

Dubrovnik Tourist Office

Ante Starčićeva 7 (020 427 591/ www.tzdubrovnik.hr). **Open** *Summer* 8am-8pm. *Winter* 9am-4pm Mon-Fri; 9am-1pm Sat.

The main tourist office near the Pile Gate has young, friendly staff – those in the much busier branch office on Stradun (020 321 561, same hours) can be quite brusque.

Atlas Travel

Brsalje 17 (020 442 574/www.atlas-croatia.com). **Open** *Summer* 8am-8pm Mon-Fri; 8am-3pm Sat. *Winter* 8am-7pm Mon-Fri; 8am-3pm Sat.
Near the Pile Gate, this travel agency books private rooms and arranges tours and excursions.

Croatian Angels

0385 62 999 999
Tourist information in English.

Croatian National Tourist Office (UK)

Croatia House, 162-164 Fulham Palace Road, London W6 9ER (020 8563 7979/www.croatia.hr).

Croatian National Tourist Office (USA)

350 Fifth Avenue, Suite 4003, New York 10118 (212 279 8672).

Tour operators & travel agencies

There are more than 100 companies who deal with Croatia. The UK Croatian National Tourist Office *(see above)* has a complete register.
adriatica.net *(+385 1 24 15 614/ www.adriatica.net).* Zagreb-based company specialising in lighthouse holidays and trips for special events.
Adventure Company *(01420 541 007/www.adventurecompany.co.uk).* Active breaks around Dalmatia: rafting; diving; canoeing; mountain biking and horse riding.
Andante Travels *(01722 713 800/ www.andantetravels.co.uk).* Archaeological tours of Dalmatia including Split, Salona and Brač.
Arblaster & Clarke Wine Tours *(01730 893 244/www.winetours.co.uk).* Wine cruises in Croatia.
Bond Tours *(01372 745 300/ www.bondtours.com).* Includes tailor-made trips, apartments, fly-drive and adventure tours.
Bosere Travel *(0143 834 094/ www.bosmeretravel.co.uk).* Specialist trips to Croatia including naturist, scuba diving, painting and trekking.

Dubrovnik Partner *Vukovarska 26 (020 448 180/www.dubrovnikpr.com).* Special events, PR, congresses and conferences in Dubrovnik.
Elite Travel *Vukovarska 17 (020 358 200/www.elite.hr).* Tours, excursions and much more.
Generalturist *Obala Stjepana Radića 24 (020 432 937/www.generalturist. com).* Eighty years' experience in local tourism – tours, tickets and travel.
Hidden Croatia *(0871 208 0075/ www.hiddencroatia.com).* City breaks and tailor-made holidays.
Holiday Options *(0870 013 0450/ www.holidayoptions.co.uk).* Large range of holidays in Croatia.
Nautilus Yachting *(01732 867 445/ www.nautilus-yachting.com).* Sailing holidays.
Saga Holidays *(0800 300 500/www. saga.co.uk).* Large list of destinations in Croatia.
Sail Croatia *(020 7751 9988/0871 733 8686/www.sailcroatia.net).* Specialists in sailing holidays from beginners upwards.
Simply Croatia *(020 8541 2214/ www.simplytravel.com).* Flights from Bristol, London and Manchester to well chosen properties in Dalmatia.
Thomson Holidays *(0870 060 0847/ www.thomson.co.uk).* Large range of holidays in Croatia.
2 Wheel Treks Cycling *(0845 612 6106/www.2wheeltreks.co.uk).* Cycling and cruise trips to Dalmatia.

Visas

Visitors from the EU, USA, Canada, Australia and New Zealand do not need a visa if staying in Croatia for less than 90 days. If you're going overland to Split from Dubrovnik, take your passport – you pass through a section of Bosnia.

What's on

The tourist office *(see above)* distributes the free monthly *Dubrovnik Guide* and *In Dubrovnik*. The website www.clubpages.net is the best source for DJ events.

Vocabulary

Pronunciation

c – 'ts' as in 'hats'
ć – a light 'ch' as 'future'
č – 'ch' as in 'church'
đ – 'dj' as in 'jury'
j – 'y' as in 'years'
š – 'sh' as in 'shoe'
ž – 'zh' as in 'pleasure'

Basics

yes *da;* no *ne*
hello/good day *dobar dan*
goodbye *do vidjenja*
hello! (familiar) *bok!*
good morning *dobro jutro*
good evening *dobra večer*
good night *laku noć*
please *molim;* thank you *hvala*
great/OK *dobro*

Useful phrases

Do you speak English?
Govorite li engleski?
Sorry, I don't speak Croatian
Izvinite, ne govorim hrvatski
I don't understand/I don't
know *Ne razumijem/ne znam*
What's your name? (polite/fam)
Kako se zovete/zoveš?
My name is... *Zovem se...*
Excuse me/sorry *Oprostite*
How much is it? *Koliko košta?*
Can I book a room? *Mogu li
rezervati sobu?*

Getting around

Where is? *Gdje je...?*
Where to? *Kamo?*
here *ovdje;* there *tamo*
left *levo;* right *desno*
straight on *pravo*
backwards *natrag*
A ticket to... *Jednu kartu za...*
single *u jednom pravcu*

return *povratnu kartu*
When does the next
bus/ferry/train leave for...?
*Kada polazi sljedeći autobus/
trajekt/vlak za...?*
I'm lost *Izgubio same se
(male)/Izgubila sam se (female)*
How far is it? *Koliko je daleko?*
arrival *polazak*
departure *odlazak*
station *kolodvor;* airport *zračna
luka;* port *luka;* ferry port
trajektna luka

Time

What time is it? *Koliko je sati?*
ten o'clock *deset sati*
day *dan;* week *tjedan*
today *danas;* tomorrow *sutra*
yesterday *jučer*
in the morning *ujutro*
in the evening *uvečer*
early *rano;* late *kasno*

Numbers

1 *jedan;* 2 *dva;* 3 *tri;* 4 *četiri;*
5 *pet;* 6 *šest;* 7 *sedam;* 8 *osam;*
9 *devet;* 10 *deset;* 20 *dvadeset;*
30 *trideset;* 40 *četrdeset;* 50
pedeset; 60 *šezdeset;* 70 *sedam-
deset;* 80 *osamdeset;* 90 *devedeset;*
100 *sto;* 200 *dvjesta;* 1,000 *tisuća*

Days, months

Monday *ponedjelak;* Tuesday
utorak; Wednesday *srijeda;*
Thursday *četvrtak;* Friday
petak; Saturday *subota;*
Sunday *nedjelja.* January *slječanj;*
February *veljača;* March *ožujak;*
April *travanj;* May *svibanj;* June
lipanj; July *srpanj;* August
kolovoz; September *rujan;*
October *listopad;* November
studeni; December *prosinac*

Menu Glossary

All Croatian menus (*jelovnik*) are usually categorised in the same way. Cold dishes (*hladna jela*) are a common starter (*predjela*), maybe Dalmatian ham or sheep's cheese. Soups (*juhe*) are generally fish (*riblja*) or beef (*govdja*). There will then be a list of *gotova jela*, dishes ready to serve, often risottos and pastas. *Specijaliteti* or *jela po narudžbi* are the specialities of the house, main courses.

Grilled dishes (*na žaru* or *sa roštilja*) include meat (*meso*), fish (*riba*) and seafood, invariably squid (*lignje*). Other main-dish preparations include stewed beef (*pašticada*) and, considered the finest delicacy, *ispod peke*. This involves braising the dish – veal, lamb and octopus are the most popular – under a bell-shaped lid (*peka*). This is then covered in hot coals so that the ingredients, juices and vegetables and all, exude flavour. The process can take up to two hours and the custom is to order well before you arrive.

Salads (*salate*) usually offered are green (*zelena*) or mixed (*mješana*), although you may be lucky and find one made with *hobotnica*, octopus. The desserts section is usually entitled *kolači* (cakes) or *slatkiši* (sweets). Drinks are *pića*, spirits *žestoka pića*.

Useful phrases

Are these seats taken? *Da li je slobodno?*
I'd like a table for two *Molim stol za dvoje*
The menu, please *Molim vas jelovnik*
Do you have...? *Imate li...?*
I'm a vegetarian *Ja sam vegetarijanac*

I'm diabetic *Ja sam dijabetičar*
large *veliko*
small *malo*
more *više*
less *manje*
expensive *skupo*
cheap *jeftino*
hot (food, drink) *toplo*
cold *hladno*
with/without *sa/bez*
I didn't order this *Nisam ovo naručio*
thank you *hvala*
The bill (please) *Račun (molim)*
Bon appetit! *Dobar tek!*
open *otvoreno*
closed *zatvoreno*

Basics (*osnovno*)

ashtray *pepeljara*
bill *račun*
bread *kruh*
cup *šalica*
fork *vilica*
glass *čaša*
knife *nož*
milk *mlijeko*
napkin *ubrus*
oil *ulje*
pepper *biber*
plate *tanjur*
salt *sol*
spoon *žlica*
sugar *šećer*
teaspoon *žličica*
vinegar *ocat*
water *voda*

Meat (*meso*)

but **leg**
govedina **beef**
grah sa svinjskom koljenicom **bean soup with pork knuckle**
guska **goose**
gusta juha **thick goulash soup**
janjetina **lamb**

jetra liver
kunićlzec rabbit
odrezak escalope (generally
veal or pork)
patka duck
piljetina chicken
prsa breast
purica/tuka turkey
srnetina venison
šunka ham
svinjetina pork
teletina veal

Fish/seafood (*riba/plodovi mora*)

grilled fish *riba sa roštilja/
na žaru*
shellfish *školjke*
bakalar dried cod
brancin sea bass
brodet fish stew
cipal golden grey mullet
dagnje/mušule/školjke mussels
hobotnica octopus
jastog lobster
kamenice/ostrige oysters
kovač John Dory
lignje squid
list sole
losos salmon
lubin sea perch
orada gilthead sea bream
oslić hake
pastrva trout
šaran carp
sipa cuttlefish
škampi scampi
trilja red mullet
tuna tuna
zubatac dentex

Accompaniments (*prilozi*)

kruh bread
krumpir potatoes
prženi krumpir chips
riža rice
tjestenina pasta

Salads (*salate*)

cikla beetroot
krastavac cucumber
mješana salata mixed salad
rajčica tomato
rokula rocket
zelena salata lettuce, green salad

Vegetables (*povrće*)

cvjetača cauliflower
gljive mushrooms
grašak peas
kuhani kukuruz sweetcorn
leća lentils
mahune green beans
mrkva carrot
paprika pepper
šparoge asparagus
špinat spinach

Fruit/nuts (*voće/orasi*)

dinja melon
jabuka apple
jagoda strawberry
kruška pear
malina raspberry
marelica apricot
naranča orange
orah walnut
šljiva plum
trešnja cherry

Drinks (*pića*)

čaj tea
kava coffee
led ice
mineralna voda mineral water
penjušac sparkling wine
pivo beer
rakija brandy (*loza* grape;
biska mistletoe; *šljivovica* plum;
travarica herb grappa;
orahovača walnut)
sok (od naranče) (orange) juice
vino wine (*crno* red; *bijelo* white;
crveno rosé; *bevanda* spritzer)

ESSENTIALS

Index

Sights & Museums

a

Adriatic Kayak Tours p99
Aquarium p47
Artur Gallery p78

b

Boninovo p91

c

Carmel Photo Gallery p78
Cathedral p47
Church of Our Lady of Mercy p107
Church of Our Saviour p47
Church of St Andrew p92
Church of St Blaise p47
Church of St George p92
Churches of St Michael in Lapad p107
Church of St Nicholas p50
Church of St Nicholas of the Shipyard p101
Church of St Peter p92
Church of St Roch p50
Church of the Holy Cross p101
City Walls Tour p50

d

Dominican Monastery p50
Dulčić, Masle, Pulitika Gallery p78

f

Franciscan Monastery p50
Franciscan Monastery Old Pharmacy Museum p53
Franjo Tudjman bridge p101

g

Galerija Sebastian p80
Gradac Park p92
Gruž p100
Gruž market p105
Gundulićeva poljana market p105

h

House of Marin Držić p54

j

Jadran cinema p80
Jesuit Church & Jesuit College p54

l

Lapad p106
Lazareti p90
Lero Theatre p80
Lovrijenac Fortress p94
Luža p54

m

Marin Držić Theatre p80
Maritime Museum p54
Mosque p54
Mount Srdj p94
Museum of Modern Art p84

o

Old Town p46
Onofrio's Fountain p55
Orthodox Church & Icon Museum p55
Our Lady of Danče p94

p

Pile p91
Pile Gate p95
Ploče p81
Ploče Gate p84

r

Rector's Palace p57
Revelin Fort p84

Rupe Ethnographic Museum p57

s

Sigurata Convent Museum p58
Sloboda cinema p80
Sponza Palace p58
Stradun p58
Synagogue p59

w

War Photo Limited p80

Eating & Drinking

a

Aè p107
Africa p59
Amfora p101
Arka p60
Atlas Club Nautika p95

b

Baracuda p60
Belfast Celtic Bar p111
Belvedere p111
Biker's Caffe p84
Bistro Riva p111
Blidinje p111
Buža I p60
Buža II p61

c

Carpe Diem p61
Casa Bar p111
Casablanca p61
Cele Café p63
Chihuahua – Cantina Mexicana p87

d

Defne p63
Domino p63
Dubrava p63
Dubrava Restaurant p87
Dubrovački kantun p63
Dundo Maroje p63

ESSENTIALS

ESSENTIALS